YORK NOTES

The Tempest

William Shakespeare

Notes by Loreto Todd

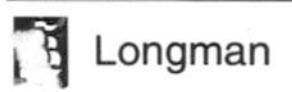

Longman

York Press

Exterior picture of the Globe Theatre reproduced by permission of the Raymond Mander and Joe Mitchenson Theatre Collection
Reconstruction of the Globe Theatre interior reprinted from Hodges; **The Globe Restored** (1968) by permission of Oxford University Press

YORK PRESS
322 Old Brompton Road, London SW5 9JH

PEARSON EDUCATION LIMITED
Edinburgh Gate, Harlow,
Essex CM20 2JE, United Kingdom
Associated companies, branches and representatives throughout the world

First published 1998
Seventh impression 2002

ISBN 0-582-32929-9

Designed by Vicki Pacey
Phototypeset by Gem Graphics, Trenance, Mawgan Porth, Cornwall
Colour reproduction and film output by Spectrum Colour
Produced by Pearson Education North Asia Limited, Hong Kong

CONTENTS

PART ONE

INTRODUCTION

HOW TO STUDY A PLAY

Studying on your own requires self-discipline and a carefully thought-out work plan in order to be effective.

- Drama is a special kind of writing (the technical term is 'genre') because it needs a performance in the theatre to arrive at a full interpretation of its meaning. Try to imagine that you are a member of the audience when reading the play. Think about how it could be presented on the stage, not just about the words on the page.
- Drama is always about conflict of some sort (which may be below the surface). Identify the conflicts in the play and you will be close to identifying the large ideas or themes which bind all the parts together.
- Make careful notes on themes, character, plot and any sub-plots of the play.
- Why do you like or dislike the characters in the play? How do your feelings towards them develop and change?
- Playwrights find non-realistic ways of allowing an audience to see into the minds and motives of their characters, for example soliloquy, aside or music. Consider how such dramatic devices are used in the play you are studying.
- Think of the playwright writing the play. Why were these particular arrangements of events, characters and speeches chosen?
- Cite exact sources for all quotations, whether from the text itself or from critical commentaries. Wherever possible find your own examples from the play to back up your opinions.
- Always express your ideas in your own words.

This York Note offers an introduction to *The Tempest* and cannot substitute for close reading of the text and the study of secondary sources.

Reading the tempest

The nature of the play

The Tempest is, at one level, a fairy tale complete with magical occurrences, suspension of the laws of nature and a happy ending, but it is much more than this. It attempts to examine the connection between suffering and purification, the supposed contrast between civilised and uncivilised people, and to illustrate, albeit briefly, the results of colonialism. The play deals with a number of serious themes but the seriousness is not allowed to cause disquiet in the audience. In spite of threats of death and disorder, the play ends on a note of triumph. The older generations have found reconciliation, and the younger ones love; Ariel has been released from his bondage and Caliban is once again master of his island.

Dramatic 'unities'

In *The Tempest*, Shakespeare adheres fairly closely to what scholars have called the 'classical unities of time, place and action'. These **unities** are based on conventions established by writers of classical Greek drama.

The unity of time implied that the length of time taken by the **action** in a play should correspond approximately to the length of time taken to perform the play. Such a correspondence was hard to maintain and so it was permissible for the imaginary action to last for a maximum of twenty-four hours. *The Tempest* can be performed in about two hours whereas its action can be calculated to span just under four. In the play, Shakespeare draws the audience's attention to the time at which certain actions occur (see I.2.238–41, V.1.3–5 and V.1.185–6).

The second unity, the unity of place, required that the scene should remain unchanged throughout the play. In *The Tempest* the entire action, with the exception of the first scene, is confined to the island.

The third unity, the unity of action, prescribed that a play which adhered to the classical unities should have only one **plot** and that all other incidents in the play should be subordinated to it. In *The Tempest* the main plot revolves around Prospero's efforts to regain his dukedom and to undo the evil which had been perpetrated against him and his daughter, Miranda.

It is impossible to say why Shakespeare chose to observe the unities in *The Tempest* when he was largely indifferent to them in his other plays.

Some **critics** have suggested that Shakespeare knew this was his last play and wanted to show that he could adhere to the classical unities when he chose. There may be some truth in this view, but it is also possible that Shakespeare simply wished to concentrate the audience's attention on the theme of reconciliation which features prominently in the play and that he found the classical unities contributed to the clarity of his presentation. Whatever his reason for observing the unities in *The Tempest*, Shakespeare was, in this play, preoccupied by the interrelated themes of sin, repentance and reconciliation, themes that Prospero directly addresses in the final scene (see V.1.25–30).

The love and harmony between Ferdinand and Miranda compensate for the quarrel and discord that separated their fathers. Because the play concentrates on evil redeemed rather than on the unhappy results of human weaknesses that are explored in such plays as *Macbeth* and *King Lear*, the setting and the behaviour are chosen more for their ability to emphasise the themes rather than for strict, naturalistic accuracy. The location of the island, for example, is never exactly specified. We are told that it is in the Mediterranean, some miles from the coast, but its exact location is less important than its ability to suggest mystery, romance and the opportunity to be alone with one's innermost thoughts. The strangeness of the island, which is at one and the same time a tropical paradise and a place where we hear of wild bulls and lions, bogs and fens, is a suitable setting for the exercise of magical charms, charms that can evoke a tempest, purge a king's guilt and allow goodness to defeat evil.

In *The Tempest*, as in his other plays, Shakespeare's use of ejaculations, oaths and references to God is conventionalised. On 27 May 1606, a statute was passed to prevent swearing in plays. According to the statute, one could be fined up to £10 (a great deal of money in the seventeenth century) for profane use of the name of God, of Jesus Christ, of the Holy Ghost or of the Trinity. *The Tempest* was written after this statute was passed and so we find that Christian references are minimised, although there are many allusions to the gods of classical mythology (see, for example, I.2.201–6).

THE NATURE OF TRAGICOMEDY

Shakespearean comedies usually treated the happier aspects of life such as love and marriage, often, as in *The Tempest*, making lavish use of music and singing. Frequently, there were two levels in the comedy, one involving the love interests of courtly characters, in this case Ferdinand and Miranda, and another dealing with the humorous behaviour of less elevated personalities, such as Trinculo and Stephano. Tragedies, however, dealt with the harsher side of life, with the trials and eventual death of an important person. Often the hero's fall from happiness was due to a weakness in his character, a weakness such as the overweening ambition of Macbeth or the uncontrolled jealousy of Othello.

In *The Tempest* we have a combination of the two types of play. Love is a central theme, as it is in such comedies as *Twelfth Night* and *As You Like It*; music is extremely important and the words of some of Ariel's songs are an integral part of the dialogue (see, for example, I.2.397–405) and yet the audience is also made aware of the less joyful possibilities of life. They are shown that evil exists. There are the seeds of possible disaster in Prospero's overthrow, in Caliban's attempt to rape Miranda, in the treatment of Caliban and Ariel, and in the plots to murder Prospero and Alonso. These seeds of doom are not allowed to develop, however, and the play ends with the reconciliation of the major characters and with the suggestion that the love between Miranda and Ferdinand has helped to compensate for the strife between their fathers.

Prose is sometimes used for comic episodes (see, for example, IV.1.194–254) whereas **blank verse** is the usual medium for more serious interaction. By alternating between prose and verse Shakespeare can emphasise differences in language and behaviour while implying the essential similarity between the needs and urges of all his characters and stressing, at the same time, the common humanity they share with their audience.

A NOTE ON MASQUES IN THE TEXT

Masques were stylised dramas incorporating poetic dialogue, music and dancing and often making lavish use of costumes, scenery and mechanical devices. They became popular as court entertainment in Elizabeth's reign and were frequently presented at the court of James I (1603–25).

Certain conventions developed in the writing and production of masques and these can be observed in the short masque that occurs in Act IV, Scene 1, lines 60–138: masques almost always dealt with classical or mythical subject matter; the characters were often gods and goddesses or personifications of abstract qualities like grace or peace; they were often composed to celebrate a marriage and so married bliss was a widely used theme; they were normally shorter than the more usual drama of the time; they frequently used rhyming couplets; and they made lavish use of music and costumes.

Occasionally, a dramatist did not use speech in the masque but employed **mime**, music, costumes and moving scenery to entertain the audience. The banquet episode in Act III, Scene 3, lines 20–52 can be regarded as a miming masque of this type.

Shakespeare's use of masques is not confined to *The Tempest*, but the appearance of two different kinds of masque in the one play may indicate the type of audience for which the play was to be performed. It may also signal the growing interest in the masque **genre** in the early part of the seventeenth century.

THE TITLE OF THE PLAY

Storms and tempests have occurred in folktales throughout recorded history. They were often used to separate natural from supernatural events, and you might like to consider whether, at its most basic level, *The Tempest* is a fairy tale. It certainly involves human beings and spirits, a handsome prince and a beautiful princess, and the triumph of good over evil. In such plays as *Othello* and *King Lear*, Shakespeare uses a storm as a means of cutting the characters off from places and people with whom they were familiar, thus making them re-examine their behaviour and their relationships. *The Tempest* uses a similar technique. It cuts the characters off from the natural world and places them on a mysterious island where love and reconciliation are magically allowed to conquer hatred and envy. The title, therefore, may refer not only to the physical storm that occurs in the first scene of the play, but to the turbulent passions of the characters, passions which, like the storm, are magically transformed into the promise of peace with which the play ends.

The Tempest was almost certainly Shakespeare's last play and it seems probable that it was written in 1611. It was performed in November 1611 at the court of King James and was apparently well received since it was again presented at the court during the winter of 1612–13 when it formed part of the entertainment provided by King James to celebrate the betrothal of his daughter Elizabeth to Frederick, the Elector of the Palatine States, in Germany.

The Tempest may not have been written specifically for the court, though it does incorporate certain courtly elements, the most obvious of which is the **masque** in Act IV (see previous section).

In writing his plays Shakespeare frequently made use of existing material, and analogues of *The Tempest* are not hard to find. It would appear, for example, that he knew Montaigne's essay 'Of Cannibals' which was published in English in 1603 and which discussed the value and the way of life of societies which had not been affected by civilisation of a European type.

It seems likely, too, that Shakespeare was affected by the many strange tales being brought back to England by travellers. In particular, he seems to have been influenced by a 1610 pamphlet called 'A Discovery of the Bermudas, other wise called the Ile of Divels'. This pamphlet described the adventures of a group of colonists travelling in a convoy of ships from London to Virginia. During the voyage, the flagship was separated from the other ships in a storm and was blown towards Bermuda. The storm tossed the ship onto the rocks but no one on board was drowned. The colonists lived on the island until they had built boats in which they could sail to Virginia. The story of their almost miraculous survival aroused considerable interest in England and echoes of their adventure can be found in *The Tempest*.

You might like to question, however, the claim that Shakespeare based his play on the pamphlet, or on Montaigne's essay or on a contemporary German play *Die Schöne Sidea* (The Lovely Sidea) which contains similar themes and events. It may seem more likely to you that Shakespeare absorbed traditional and contemporary material and created a play which is not identical in character or treatment with any of his sources.

Part two

Summaries

The Tempest *was originally printed in the First* ***Folio*** *of 1623 and it is remarkably free from inaccuracies and inconsistencies. As well as paying close attention to the language of the play, the Folio editor divides the play into* ***acts*** *and scenes and provides detailed stage directions. All subsequent editions of* The Tempest *have been based on the text of the First Folio although the spelling has been modernised so that 'have', for example, appears as* have *and not as* haue. *The main differences between modern texts is in the numbering of lines. The acts and scenes are the same but the prose text differs in length depending on the size of the font and the width of the page. Since most of the play is, however, written in* ***blank verse****, the line numbering is not radically different. The text quoted in this book is from the Arden edition of the works of William Shakespeare.* The Tempest *is edited by Frank Kermode and published by Methuen and Co. Ltd, London, 1966.*

Synopsis

The play opens with a storm at sea. Alonso, the King of Naples, is sailing home after the marriage of his daughter, Claribel, to the King of Tunis. During the voyage, the weather suddenly deteriorates and Alonso's ship is separated from the rest of the fleet and driven towards an island. The ship hits the coastal rocks and all the passengers leap overboard in the hope of swimming ashore. From this point onward, all the **action** occurs on the island.

In the second scene, we meet Prospero, who had once been the Duke of Milan. Prospero explains to his daughter, Miranda, how he had been more interested in books than in safeguarding his position, and so had lost his dukedom twelve years earlier. He had been overthrown by his brother, Antonio, who had received help and support from King Alonso. Antonio and Alonso had ordered an old nobleman, Gonzalo, to abandon Prospero and his young daughter at sea in a leaky boat. Gonzalo, however, had taken pity on them and had provided them with food, drink, clothing and Prospero's beloved books. Prospero and Miranda had been washed ashore on the island and had found one human inhabitant there, a boy of twelve called Caliban. The boy's mother, a witch called Sycorax, had died soon after she had been banished to the island by the ruler of Algiers. At first, Prospero liked Caliban and decided to educate him, but his affection turned to anger when Caliban attempted to rape Miranda. Prospero punished Caliban by enslaving him. Prospero had also found a spirit called Ariel on the island. Ariel had been imprisoned in a tree by Sycorax but Prospero studied his books and learned how to set Ariel free by magic. Prospero freed the spirit but only when Ariel had promised to obey him. Ariel had been obeying one of Prospero's commands when he had caused the storm and apparent shipwreck.

Still under instructions from Prospero, Ariel lures Alonso's son away from the members of his party and leads him towards Prospero's cell. When Ferdinand sees Miranda, he thinks she is a goddess, and Miranda, who has previously only seen her father and Caliban, is equally attracted to the young prince. Prospero is pleased to see that his plan to bring the young people together is working and decides to strengthen their love by putting difficulties in the way of its fulfilment. Accordingly, in spite of Miranda's pleas for mercy, Ferdinand is apprehended as a prisoner and condemned to carry logs.

In the meantime, Alonso believes that his son has been drowned and is filled with grief. Gonzalo tries to console the king but Alonso is irritated by what he regards as false optimism. Their search for Ferdinand has exhausted them and they are forced to lie down and rest. While they are asleep, Antonio, the current Duke of Milan, suggests to Sebastian that they could kill Alonso and seize his throne. Ariel, however, has heard their plotting and wakes Gonzalo up in time. Antonio and Sebastian explain that they had drawn their swords to protect the sleeping party from wild animals. Their story is believed and the royal party moves off to continue the search for Ferdinand.

On another part of the island, Caliban meets two of the shipwrecked men: Trinculo, the jester, and Stephano, the butler. Stephano gives him some alcohol and Caliban assumes that he must be a god if he possesses such heavenly liquid. Caliban offers to serve Stephano and make him lord of the island if he agrees to kill Prospero. The three set off to find Prospero but Ariel becomes aware of the plot, lures them into a stagnant pool where they are trapped up to their necks in mud, and goes to tell Prospero about the plot.

Alonso's party fails to find Ferdinand but they encounter some spirits who lay out a feast for them. Before they can eat it, however, Ariel disguises himself as a harpy, that is, a mythological character with the body of a woman but the wings and claws of a bird, and reminds them of their sins against Prospero twelve years ago. The feast suddenly disappears and Alonso is overcome by remorse. Antonio and Sebastian are, however, unmoved by Ariel's account of their evil actions.

Prospero watches the manly way that Ferdinand attempts to carry out his punishment and is sufficiently impressed by the young prince's behaviour to agree to his marriage to Miranda. He provides a wedding **masque** to mark their union but, towards the end of it, he remembers Caliban's plan to kill him. The three plotters are pursued by spirits who have taken on the shape of large, fierce hounds.

By the last act of the play Prospero has achieved all that he set out to do: he has shown Alonso, Antonio and Sebastian that they had committed a crime against him in banishing him from Milan; they ask for his forgiveness and his dukedom is restored to him. Prospero reveals to Alonso that his son is alive and the friendship between Alonso and Prospero is sealed by the marriage of Ferdinand and Miranda. Prospero frees Ariel and decides to renounce his magical powers. The boatswain brings news that, in spite of the storm, the ship is seaworthy and ready for the journey to Italy.

In the **Epilogue**, Prospero renounces his magic and asks the audience to release him from their spell by the power of their applause.

ACT I

SCENE 1 On a ship at sea during a wild storm. There is noise and confusion everywhere as sailors and passengers struggle to survive

Most of the **action** of the play takes place on an island. The first scene, however, is a realistic recreation of the dangers of a storm at sea. The ship in distress is carrying Alonso, the king of Naples, from Tunisia where he and his party had been celebrating his daughter's marriage. The master of the ship encourages the boatswain to do all in his power to save the ship but, while he is struggling, he is interrupted by the royal party. The boatswain knows that they can do nothing to help and so he orders them back to their cabin. Gonzalo tries to comfort the king and his companions by pointing out that the boatswain has the face of a man who is doomed to be hanged and that, if there is any truth in the proverb, 'A man who is born to be hanged will never be drowned', then none of them will perish in the sea. Alonso returns to his cabin but three of the other nobles stay on deck and get in the boatswain's way. He warns them that their interference may lead to everyone's death. They are not convinced that the boatswain is fully in control and so they jump overboard in an attempt to swim to the shore.

The setting of a storm at sea is a dramatically effective opening. In addition, it provides the audience with a **metaphor** for the past turmoil in the lives of the characters and carries the suggestion, perhaps, that 'after the storm comes the calm'. Shakespeare often uses a storm in his plays as a prelude to a transition from one phase of life to another. We find storms, for example, in *King Lear*, *Macbeth*, *Othello* and *Twelfth Night* and most members of the audience would have been aware of the significance of tempests in the **Bible** (see Imagery and Symbolism).

Boatswain the sailor in charge of the equipment on a ship. The word is pronounced and sometimes written 'bosun', as it is in line 12

What cheer? is there any good news?

yarely quickly, smartly

Bestir get a move on

Heigh, my hearts come on, mates

cheerly don't be depressed

Yare be quick

tend to pay attention to

Blow till thou burst thy wind blow until you blow yourself out. (The boatswain is addressing the storm.)

Play the men give directions to the sailors

mar our labour get in the way of our work

Nay, good no, my good man

When the sea is I'll be patient when the sea is calm
roarers winds and waves
To cabin go to your cabin
thou Gonzalo uses 'thou' to the boatswain, indicating that he is inferior in rank to the nobles. The boatswain uses 'you' to the nobles
councillor a wise man, a member of the king's council
If you can command these elements to silence if you can stop the storm
hand a rope more handle another rope (in an effort to control the sails)
mischance bad luck
if it so hap if it is going to happen
Methinks I believe
His complexion is perfect gallows judging by his appearance, he is born to die on the gallows, that is, he will be hanged
Stand fast, good Fate, to his hanging let's hope that his fate is to hang
Make the rope of his destiny our cable let the rope that will hang him prove to be our lifeline. In other words, if he outlives this storm, so do we
our own doth little advantage our own fate does not look bright at the moment
topmast the mast above
Bring her to try with main-course use the mainsail to steady the ship, that is, sail close to the wind so that the sails will not be brought down
A plague upon this howling damn them for making so much noise. The boatswain cannot concentrate because of the noise made by the courtiers
our office the instructions I give. The boatswain suggests that the courtiers are making more noise than the storm, with the result that his orders cannot be heard
What do you here? what are you doing here?
give o'er give up, stop trying to save the ship
pox venereal disease. Sebastian's curse is a strong one
blasphemous swearing, using God's name profanely
incharitable uncharitable, uncaring
Work you, then you do the work, then! The boatswain is, in effect, telling Sebastian to save the ship himself or else to shut up
cur dog
whoreson bastard, son of a woman of loose morals
I'll warrant him for drowning I'll guarantee that this man will not drown
unstanched wench incontinent young woman
Lay her a-hold bring the ship close to the wind

Set her two courses get the mainsail and the topsail in the right positions
All lost we and everyone will be drowned
What, must our mouths be cold? the boatswain's question has two meanings: 'Must we die?' and 'Must we face such danger without a drink of rum?' The second meaning seems to be the one understood by Antonio who, three lines later, claims that they will drown because of the incompetence of drunken sailors
our case is as theirs we are all in the same danger
wide-chapped big mouthed. Perhaps this implies that he drinks too much
The washing of ten tides it was customary in Shakespeare's day for the bodies of pirates to be left hanging on the shore until three tides had come in and gone out. This punishment was meant to be a warning to others of the dangers of piracy. Antonio thinks the boatswain is such a criminal that his body should be exposed to ten tides
He'll be hanged yet ... glut him the boatswain will be hanged as a criminal even though it looks as if he will drown. He will hang and his body will be left to swallow so much water that he will burst
We split the ship is breaking up
furlong one eighth of a mile, approximately 200 metres. Gonzalo is suggesting that he would exchange the entire ocean for one small piece of dry land
The wills above be done I accept the will of God
would fain die a dry death would prefer to die on dry land

SCENE 2 Outside Prospero's cell on the island. The audience is introduced to the remaining characters and provided with all the background information necessary to understand their actions and motivations

This very long scene is a means of explaining the background of the play to the audience. It takes place on the island on which the ship has been wrecked. The first inhabitants we meet are Miranda and her father, Prospero. Miranda has seen the shipwreck and asks her father to help the victims, especially if he is responsible for causing the storm. Prospero assures her that no harm has come to anyone and that he has used his magical powers entirely for her sake. Then he tells her their history. Twelve years earlier, when Miranda was not quite three years old, he, Prospero, was the Duke of Milan. He had always loved books and had gradually devoted more and more of his time to study, leaving the task of ruling Milan to his brother, Antonio. Slowly but surely, Antonio assumed increased powers until he was in full control of Milan in all but name. In a bid to take over the dukedom completely, Antonio appealed to King Alonso of Naples. He offered to pay Alonso an annual tribute in return for the king's help in dislodging Prospero. Alonso agreed and sent an army to help Antonio to depose Prospero.

Miranda asks why she and her father were not killed. Prospero tells her that Antonio and Alonso had refrained from killing them because they were afraid of the reaction of the Milanese people, who had always loved him. However, the insurgents condemned Prospero and Miranda to be cast adrift in an old, unseaworthy vessel without sail or oar, in the expectation that they would die at sea. Fortunately, a nobleman called Gonzalo supplied them with food, water, clothing and, most important of all in Prospero's eyes, his beloved books. Because of Gonzalo's help, they had managed to reach their present island and, as soon as they were established there, Prospero was determined to have the upper hand. At this stage in the narrative, Prospero puts Miranda into a deep sleep so that the spirit Ariel can tell him what has been happening.

Ariel reports that he has obeyed Prospero's commands to the letter. He has separated Alonso's ship from the rest of the fleet, causing them to believe that the king and his party have drowned. He has frightened the courtiers so that they have abandoned ship. He has seen to it that each one of them is safe although their party has been split up. In particular, Alonso's son Ferdinand is alone, as Prospero had instructed, the ship is safe in the harbour and the crew is asleep.

Ariel asks Prospero for his freedom and Prospero accuses him of ingratitude. Years before Prospero had arrived on the island, a witch called Sycorax had been banished there from Algeria. While on the island, she had given birth to a son, Caliban, and had imprisoned Ariel in a pine tree. Ariel had been imprisoned in the tree for twelve years, during which time Sycorax had died, and he would have been left in the tree forever if Prospero had not released him. Ariel is told that he must continue to obey his master or risk being imprisoned in an oak tree. Ariel promises to be obedient and Prospero assures him that, if he does all that is required of him, he will be given his freedom within two days.

When Ariel leaves, Prospero wakens Miranda and suggests that they go to see Caliban. Miranda does not like Caliban and does not want to visit him. However, at that moment, he appears carrying firewood for Prospero. Prospero treats Caliban as a slave by day and sends spirits to torment him by night. Caliban curses Prospero and Miranda, claiming that the island had been his until Prospero had used his magic to take it away from him. Caliban insists that Prospero is not only ruthless but hypocritical. When he had first arrived on the island, he had befriended Caliban, teaching him to speak. Caliban had, in return, shared his knowledge of the island with Prospero but Prospero had enslaved him. Prospero insists that Caliban had repaid his early kindness by trying to rape Miranda and Caliban's answer is that he only regrets that the attempted rape had been unsuccessful. Caliban is totally dominated by Prospero.

Ferdinand is lured to Prospero's cave by Ariel's singing. There, he meets Miranda and her father. Ferdinand and Miranda fall in love immediately and Ferdinand, thinking that his father is dead, offers to make her the queen of Naples. Prospero, who had planned the meeting and hoped that the young couple would love each other, decides that Ferdinand must suffer for Miranda. Otherwise, he might not value her highly enough. Accordingly, he uses his magical powers to imprison Ferdinand, and Ferdinand feels that his imprisonment will be worthwhile if it enables him to see Miranda. Miranda is upset with her father but feels certain that Ferdinand's imprisonment will not last long.

Islands have often been selected by writers as a means of allowing characters to develop in isolation. Such a setting was employed by Daniel Defoe for *Robinson Crusoe* (1719) and, more recently, by William Golding in *Lord of the Flies* (1954). Shakespeare also uses the theme of one brother being usurped by another in *As You Like It*. In this latter play, the senior brother lives with some followers in the Forest of Arden but also regains his dukedom.

Art magical powers

allay weaken, make them less powerful

stinking pitch the sky was so dark that it looked as if tar, and not rain, would fall from it

mounting to the welkin's cheek rising up to the sky

welkin sky

creature person

perished died by drowning
I would have sunk ... within her if I had been a god, I would have caused the earth to swallow up the sea rather than allow the ship to sink with all its passengers and crew still on board
fraughting souls the human freight
Be collected don't be upset
amazement terror, horror
piteous compassionate
in care of thee out of consideration for you
who art ignorant of what thou art who do not know who you really are
whence I am where I've come from
more better very much better than I seem. This is an emphatic comparative
full poor cell very mediocre dwelling place
And thy no greater father and nothing more than simply your father
did never meddle with my thoughts never entered my mind
inform thee further tell you more about yourself
Lie there my Art Prospero is addressing his gown, which is a **symbol** of his magic powers
direful spectacle of the wrack terrible image of the shipwreck
virtue very essence
provision foresight
not so much perdition as an hair has not lost even one hair from their head. There are many references to the **Bible** in this play. This one would have reminded an Elizabethan audience of St Luke's gospel (12:7), where Jesus tells his followers that God loves them so much that 'the very hairs of your head are all numbered'
Betid happened to
bootless inquisition useless questioning
Stay wait
cell small, simple room
Out three years old quite three years old
By what? what can you remember?
with thy remembrance in your memory
assurance certainty
tended me served and looked after me
In the dark backward in the dimly remembered past
abysm bottomless pit, abyss

aught anything
How thou cam'st here thou mayst you may remember how you came here
twelve year since twelve years ago
a piece of virtue a perfect example of virtuous womanhood
no worse issued equally nobly born
What foul play had we what evil was done to us
thence that place
Or bless'd was't we did? or was it a good thing that we left?
holp hither helped to get here
teen trouble, pain, grief
from my remembrance faded from my memory
Please you, farther please tell me more
mark me pay close attention
perfidious treacherous, unfaithful
next thyself after you
put the manage of my state gave him the power to manage Milan
signories dukedoms, states. Prospero is claiming that Milan was the most prosperous of all the states of northern Italy
prime duke highest ranking duke
reputed famed, respected
liberal arts the arts and knowledge necessary to a man of such rank
cast upon gave responsibility to
to my state grew stranger gradually became less and less involved in affairs of state
rapt in secret studies involved in private studies. There may be a suggestion here that Prospero was studying magic
most heedfully very attentively
being perfected having learnt the art of
grant suits give certain people what they wanted
deny refuse
trash for over-topping check because he was becoming too ambitious
new created remade in his own likeness
the key the means to control. The word 'key' has two meanings here: a mechanism for opening and closing, and the key in which a tune is sung or played
ivy which had hid my princely trunk Antonio gradually replaced me
verdure vigour, vitality, health. If the ivy covers a tree completely, it can kill it

Thou attend'st not you are not paying attention
I thus neglecting Prospero tells Miranda that he neglected the affairs of state in order to devote himself to his studies; that he trusted his brother completely and gave him absolute power; that the power brought out the faults in Antonio's character; and that Antonio's evil was in sharp contrast to Prospero's generosity
closeness seclusion, isolation
sans bound without boundaries, limitless. *Sans* is from French but was quite widely used in Shakespeare's day to mean 'without'. It was pronounced to rhyme with 'bans'
lorded elevated to the rank of lord
what my power might else extract anything else that could be gained by the use of my position
Who having into truth ... duke who had lied to himself so often that he began to believe that he was the duke
prerogative the rights and powers associated with rank
would cure deafness Miranda's humorous reply is an emphatic way of stressing how attentively she is listening
screen barrier, impediment
Absolute Milan the duke of Milan in fact
temporal royalties the work of state, the ability to rule
confederates conspires
so dry he was for sway he was so eager for control
subject his coronet to his crown put the dukedom of Milan under the power of the throne of Naples
yet unbowed never before subjected to an outside power
his condition (1) the sort of person he is and (2) the arrangement he came to
the event the result
an enemy to me inveterate being a longstanding enemy of mine
hearkens to listens to and agrees with
in lieu o' the premises in return for the terms of the agreement made
presently immediately
extirpate banish, get rid of
levied raised quickly
fated to arranged for
ministers for the purpose people who had been appointed to carry out the plan
a hint that wrings mine eyes an event that causes me to cry copiously

Which now's upon's that is happening now
impertinent irrelevant
Wherefore why
wench young woman
durst not did not dare
With colours fairer painted their foul ends they hid their evil action
In few in brief
bark small ship
a rotten carcass of a butt a shell of a boat that was no better than a tub
not rigged without sails
hoist us left us to drift
cherubin a small angel
Thou wast what did preserve me you were the reason I survived
infused filled with
decked covered, added to
burthen burden, weighty troubles
undergoing stomach the courage and ability to endure
Providence divine divine providence, the kindness of God
charity loving kindness, generosity
being then appointed ... this design having been put in charge of the plan to get rid of us
steaded us helped us greatly
furnished supplied
made thee more profit provided you with a better education
beating in my mind troubling me
Know thus far forth I'll tell you this much
Fortune luck was (and still is) personified as a woman, cf. Lady Luck
prescience foresight, planning
zenith the highest point, the period when a person is luckiest
A most auspicious star a reference to the widely-held belief that our lives and fortunes are influenced by the movements of the stars and planets
If now I court not if I do not immediately seize this opportunity
Thou art inclined to sleep: it is probable that Prospero is using his powers to make his daughter sleep
give it way allow it (the drowsiness) to have its way; sleep
Come away come in
answer thy best pleasure to do what you want me to do

be't to fly whether it is to fly
all his quality all the other spirits
performed to point the tempest created the storm exactly as I told you to
to every article to the last detail
beak front of the ship
waist the central section of the ship
flamed amazement brought terror to everyone by the flames I caused
yards the long beams that are used for suspending the sails
bowsprit pole that helps to support the sails and ropes
Jove the king of the Roman gods
precursors forerunners
Neptune Roman god of the sea. Neptune was usually depicted carrying a trident and blowing a horn
besiege attack
coil tumult, uproar
infect his reason cause him to go mad
all but mariners everyone except the crew
the foaming brine the raging waters
quit abandoned
all afire with me which seemed to be on fire because of my actions
upstaring standing on end because of fear
nigh shore near the shore
sustaining garments supporting clothes. The clothes became buoyant and kept them afloat
blemish mark
as thou bad'st me as you ordered
troops small groups
odd angle remote corner
sad knot folded. It is likely that Ariel folds his arms to show how Ferdinand is sitting
say how thou has disposed tell me what you've done with
the still-vexed Bermoothes the perpetually stormy Bermudas
under hatches stowed kept below deck
with a charm to their suffered labour adding a spell to the hard work they had to perform
flote sea
wracked destroyed by the storm

his great person and the king himself
thy charge Exactly is performed you have done your work perfectly
mid season noon
at least two glasses at least two o'clock. Hours were measured by an hour-glass
'twixt six and now between now and six o'clock
preciously carefully and fully
give me pains give me additional hard work
remember thee remind you
performed me given to me
before the time be out before the appointed time
prithee beg you
made no mistakings made no mistakes
or ... or either ... or
to bate me let me off, abate my service
thinkst it much you think it such a lot
the veins o' th' earth the underground waterways
malignant evil, corrupt
forgot forgotten
the foul witch Sycorax Sycorax was Caliban's mother. She represents a type of female spirit found in several folk cultures and thought to lure men to their deaths
grown into a hoop bent over so that her chin almost met her feet
Argier Algeria
mischiefs manifold many sins
sorceries terrible appalling acts of magic
for one thing she did because of one action. Perhaps Sycorax was not killed because she was pregnant. In Shakespeare's day, a woman, who was due to be hanged was let off the death sentence if she was pregnant
blue-eyed possibly, with dark blue shadows under the eyes
for thou wert because you were
hests commands
potent ministers strong servants
cloven pine split pine tree
vent thy groans called out in pain
litter give birth to. The use of 'litter' suggests that Caliban is little more than an animal

whelp pup, young of an animal
Caliban There are many possible interpretations of this name. It may be an anagram of 'canibal' or a form of 'Caribbean' or from Italian *calibro*, 'mould'
in service as a servant
more murmur'st complain any further
peg thee lock you up, imprison you
correspondent obedient
gently as carefully and as correctly as I can
discharge free
nymph spirit of nature, usually a female spirit
with diligence quickly
heaviness weariness
miss do without, manage without his help
serves in offices performs all sorts of tasks
hark in thine ear let me whisper in your ear
got by the devil fathered by the devil
dam mother. The word is normally used of an animal
ravens these birds were often associated with witchcraft
south-west the winds from the south-west were supposed to bring sickness
pen thy breath make it difficult for you to breathe
urchins hedgehogs or spirits in the form of hedgehogs
for that vast of night throughout the long night
by Sycorax left to me by Sycorax, my mother
the bigger light the sun
qualities attributes, beauties
sty me make me live like a pig
stripes may move may be influenced only by beatings
any print of goodness Prospero claims that goodness makes no impact on Caliban
race inherited nature
rid destroy. Caliban wishes that Prospero might die from the plague
hag-seed child of a witch
rack thee with old cramps cause you to suffer from pains associated with age
Setebos the name given to a South American god
whist made quiet
featly daintily, gracefully
burthen chorus or refrain of a song, usually spelt 'burden'

passion deeply-felt sorrow
ditty does remember the words remind me of
the earth owes is earthly, belongs to this world
The fringed curtains ... advance raise your eyelids, open your eyes
canker cancer, something that can destroy beauty
bear me conduct myself, behave
maid (1) unmarried, (2) human
a single thing totally alone
Naples the king of Naples
mine eyes ne'er since at ebb my eyes have not stopped weeping
his brave son This line suggests that Antonio had a son, but he is not mentioned again in the play
control contradict
your affection not gone forth your love not given to someone else
both in either's power totally in love, absorbed in each other
uneasy difficult
attend me listen to me
name thou ow'st not a title that does not belong to you
fresh-brook mussels fresh-water mussels were virtually inedible
entertainment treatment
my foot my tutor Shall I take instructions from an inferior?
come from thy ward don't try to defend yourself with your sword
impostor liar, one who pretends to be the king of Naples
goodlier better, more handsome
nerves sinews, muscles
unwonted unusual

Act II

SCENE 1 **Another part of the island. The audience learns more about the shipwrecked passengers and about Antonio's lack of remorse for his crime against Prospero. Ariel prevents the murder of Alonso**

The **action** now moves to the part of the island where Alonso and his party have been washed ashore. Alonso is depressed because he believes that his son, Ferdinand, has been drowned. He finds little consolation in Gonzalo's suggestions that Ferdinand may still be alive and that their own survival is something to be grateful for. Gonzalo philosophises on the ideal state, a type of 'commonwealth' where labour and rewards are equally shared by all members of the community. Alonso finds the old man's comments tiresome, but Antonio and Sebastian mock Gonzalo both for his views and for the dull way he expresses them.

Ariel, who is invisible to the castaways, casts a spell on them to make them drowsy. They all fall asleep except for Antonio and Sebastian. Seeing how unprotected Alonso is, Antonio urges Sebastian to seize his chance, kill Alonso and take his brother's throne for himself, in the same way that he, Antonio, had usurped Prospero and become the Duke of Milan.

Sebastian succumbs to Antonio's temptation. He offers to kill Gonzalo if Antonio kills Alonso and he promises Antonio that the tribute he pays to Naples will be cancelled once Alonso is dead. Before they can carry out the murders, however, Ariel sings in Gonzalo's ear, waking him up. Gonzalo rouses the king who demands to know why Sebastian and Antonio have their swords out. Sebastian and Antonio pretend that they had drawn their swords to protect their sleeping companions from wild animals. Their explanation is accepted and the group sets out in search of Ferdinand.

> One of the themes of the play is relationships: between brothers (Antonio and Prospero, Alonso and Sebastian); between fathers and children (Prospero and Miranda, Alonso and Ferdinand); between 'masters' and 'slaves' (Prospero and Ariel, Prospero and Caliban); between men and women (Caliban and Miranda, Ferdinand and Miranda).

Beseech you I beg you

our hint of woe the cause of our problem

like cold porridge Sebastian's comment is ambiguous. He may mean that the comfort being provided by Gonzalo is valueless or that Alonso is not in the mood to be comforted. Either way, he and Antonio show little sympathy for the sufferings of others. They joke with each other throughout the scene
visitor a person who visits the sick and troubled in order to provide comfort
One: tell That's the first attempt; keep count
entertainer person who receives the grief
dolour sorrow. Sebastian is **punning** on the similarity of sound between the coin and the sorrow and thus deliberately making fun of Gonzalo, whom he regards as a windbag
wiselier more intelligently
spare stop trying to console me
crow speak. Antonio and Sebastian bet on whether Adrian, the young cock, or Gonzalo, the old cockerel, will speak first. Sebastian loses
desert uninhabited
temperance mild climate. Antonio deliberately misunderstands Adrian and takes Temperance to be a woman's name. In the early seventeenth century, Puritans often gave children the names of virtues, such as Charity, Faith or Temperance
a subtle a crafty one too
vouched so-called
their freshness and glosses their newness and shine. There is a suggestion here that, since the clothes seem to have benefited from being immersed in the water, the people may also benefit. The men may be re-baptised by the experience
sweet marriage The information about the marriage helps the audience to understand the reasons for the voyage. Since Sebastian is being sarcastic about the benefits of the return journey, it is possible that he is suggesting that the marriage may not be as happy as Gonzalo suggests
Dido the queen of Carthage at the time of the Trojan Wars. Dido fell in love with Aeneas, the founder of Rome. They got married and she committed suicide when he left her
Tunis ... Carthage Gonzalo claims that Tunis was built on the site of Carthage
the wall According to a Greek legend, the walls of Thebes rose when a god played a harp. Antonio jokes that Gonzalo has just performed a similar miracle by raising the walls of Carthage in Tunis

kernels pips. Gonzalo is mocked throughout this scene. The suggestion is that he will take the island home in his pocket, like an apple, and use its seeds to plant other islands
bate with the exception of
in a sort in a way, up to a point
in my rate in my opinion
the surges the surging waves
loose her give her up to. There is just the suggestion here of the **plot** of *Othello*, where Desdemona, the Venetian, marries Othello, the Moor or North African
loathness lack of desire to marry. Sebastian cruelly adds to his brother's grief
So is ... the loss And my loss is the greatest
chirurgeonly surgeon-like
plantation Gonzalo uses the word to mean 'colonisation' but Sebastian and Antonio choose to misinterpret him and assume he means 'planting'
commonwealth a nation in which wealth and property are equally distributed. This play raises many of the issues of colonisation that were being discussed at the time
by contraries contrary to what is normally done
name title
Letters education, learning. All people would be equal. This attitude contrasts sharply with Prospero's actions on the island
succession inheritance of land, property, wealth
bourn boundary
tilth tilling the land
No sovereignty no monarchy. Gonzalo is, however, explaining what he would do if he were king!
engine mechanism of war
foison abundant harvest
Save his Majesty the 'God' is omitted because of laws forbidding swearing
nothing nonsense
minister occasion give an opportunity for laughing
sensible sensitive. Gonzalo is making the point that Antonio and Sebastian regularly mock him
flat-long using the flat part of the sword, suggesting that Gonzalo's wit has missed its mark

sphere a reference to the system of astronomy described by Ptolemy. According to the Ptolemaic system, the moon, sun and stars circled the earth, each in its own fixed sphere. The reference to 'flat' above might also be seen as a reinforcement of the once commonly held view that the earth was flat
bat-fowling catching birds by mesmerising them with a bright light
adventure my discretion so weakly risk my reputation for discretion so easily
guard your person Sebastian and Antonio promise to guard the king in much the same way that Macbeth promises to guard King Duncan. Regicide was always regarded as a serious sin, but doubly so when treachery was involved
Th'occasion speaks thee the opportunity (to seize the throne) is calling out to you
Noble Sebastian **dramatic irony**. There is no nobility in murderous thoughts
wink'st/Whiles you have your eyes closed while
if heed me if you pay attention to me
trebles thee o'er makes you three times as important as you are now
standing water this may be a reference to the proverb 'Still water runs deep'. Sebastian is claiming that he is so far unmoved by Antonio's suggestions
To ebb/Heriditary sloth instructs me natural laziness or my position as second son suggests that I should move back from such suggestions
setting set, fixed look
a matter something of considerable significance
lord of weak remembrance Gonzalo, whose memory is poor
earthed buried
Professes to persuade is only trying to console Alonso because he does not really believe that Ferdinand is alive
hope Antonio plays on the word 'hope'. Believing that Ferdinand is dead allows him to hope that his ambitions will be fulfilled. Ambition cannot aim for anything higher than a throne and yet not even ambition can see into the future. Antonio is responsible for planting the notion of murder in Sebastian's head but Sebastian is quick to respond
Ten leagues beyond too far away from Naples to be a serious contender for the throne
unless the sun were post unless the sun acted as a messenger
cast again thrown up on the shore. The use of 'cast' is a reference to fate. Antonio suggests that fate has given them an opportunity to advance themselves and that the future is in their hands
cubit approximately half a metre or the length from the finger tips to the

elbow. There is **dramatic irony** in the choice of 'cubit' because it was used in the sixteenth century to translate the point made in St Matthew's Gospel (6:27) about a man not being able to change his height by thinking about it
say this were death supposing they were now dead
There be there are others who
chough of as deep chat jackdaw that could talk as well as Gonzalo
I remember it is clear that Sebastian realises that he is being invited to usurp Alonso
feater more gracefully. Antonio suggests he has done well since usurping Prospero
fellows equals
men servants
conscience Antonio claims that his conscience does not bother him but, if it did, he would deal with it as if it were a chilblain on his foot
candied be they consciences can be sweetened
perpetual wink everlasting sleep, death. Antonio shows no respect for Gonzalo's age or wisdom
tell the clock agree to whatever we say
free thee from thy tribute when you've killed Alonso, you'll have no further tribute to pay to Naples
I the king Sebastian already sees himself as king
for else his project dies otherwise his plan is ruined
sudden quick
securing your repose ensuring your safety while you slept
humming Gonzalo remembers Ariel's whispering in his ear
verily true

SCENE 2 Another part of the island. The scene provides details about the original island dwellers

In this scene, the audience is encouraged to focus on Caliban. Caliban is cursing Prospero, who makes him carry firewood by day and sends spirits to torment him by night. When he sees Alonso's court jester, Trinculo, he thinks that he must be one of Prospero's spirits and decides to hide in the hope that he will avoid more pain. Trinculo has swum ashore and is looking for somewhere to hide from the rain. When he sees Caliban's cloak, he thinks it is some strange outcrop on the island and he crawls under it for shelter.

Alonso's butler, Stephano, comes along and sees a cloak on the ground with four legs sticking out of it. Stephano had reached the island by clinging to a barrel of wine and it is clear that he has already had a lot to drink. He questions the 'thing' on the ground and is amazed when Trinculo answers. After some knock-about farce, Trinculo and Caliban reveal themselves and Stephano shares his wine with them. It is Caliban's first taste of alcohol and he believes that the man who can provide such heavenly liquid must be a god. He offers to serve Stephano in the hope that Stephano will free him from Prospero's yoke. The three move off drunkenly so that Caliban can show them the treasures of his island.

This scene encourages the audience to think about colonisation. In thinking about this subject, we must be careful to avoid **anachronisms**. We know a great deal about the evils of slavery and the problems associated with colonisation. When Shakespeare wrote this play, however, British colonisation was in its infancy, with settlers in Ireland and North and South America only. In addition, few writers of the day questioned the rights of Europeans to colonise other countries.

Prospero has enslaved Caliban in the way that many colonising countries enslaved the people of the countries they 'discovered'. The Nigerian writer, Chinua Achebe, writes about Europeans who claimed to have 'discovered' Nigeria in the fifteenth century, pointing out that, for the local people, Nigeria had never been lost.

inch-meal little by little, inch by inch

urchin-shows apparitions of spirits, goblins

firebrand will o' the wisp. Caliban lists the torments he has been subjected to

mow make faces, grimace

wound surrounded by, intertwined with

mind notice, pay attention to

bear off shelter from

bombard a large leather container for holding liquids, often alcohol

Poor-John a fish, usually hake, that is cured to disguise the fact that it is going off

Were I ... silver Trinculo suggests that if he were at home and had even a painting of this fish-like 'creature', he would display it outside a booth at a fair and everyone would pay to go inside and stare at the monster. The references here and in the following lines give some indication of the treatment of people of other cultures. They were often taken to Europe and treated like exotic animals for people to pay and stare at

make a man make a fortune for a man

doit coin of very little value. The reference here is to beggars on the street. Elizabeth I (d.1603) had issued proclamations to encourage the repatriation of 'Irish' and 'Blackamoor' beggars

dead Indian Native Americans were occasionally displayed at fairs to the curious. Often, the Indians did not survive long and so the dead bodies were 'exhibited'

legged with legs

gaberdine cloak, outer garment

Misery acquaints ... bedfellows in extreme conditions, one can put up with a lot

shroud cover myself

dregs last part. Much of Trinculo's **imagery** is related to drinking

at a man's funeral drinking was not uncommon at wakes. Stephano may be thinking of the death of his companions or the fact that he himself almost died

swabber man who cleaned or swabbed the decks

tang sting. Stephano **puns** on 'tongue' and 'tang'

itch The song refers to sexual desires and perhaps to the effects of sexually transmitted diseases. Scabies, a skin infection and not a sexually-transmitted disease, was also sometimes called 'the itch'

Do you put tricks upon's are you trying to frighten me?

Ind India or the West Indies

proper handsome, fine

ague a fever resembling malaria

recover bring him round, cause him to recover

neat's leather cow's hide, cow's leather

after the wisest very intelligently

trembling trembling was often thought of as a prelude to demonic possession

here is that ... cat this is a reference to the proverb: 'Ale can make a cat talk'

shake your shaking make you stop shaking, either with fear or fever

Open your chaps open your mouth

detract related to the sin of 'detraction', speaking the truth about someone in order to injure their character

ACT II SCENE 2 continued

long spoon a reference to another proverb 'If you eat with the devil, you will need a long spoon'. This means that it is imperative to think before taking action
siege of this moon-calf seat for this strange creature. Deformities in humans and animals was often explained by suggesting that they were conceived when the moon was full
vent excrete
butt of sack barrel of wine
kiss the book have a drink. The suggestion is that the bottle is like a bible
goose the meaning is not clear. It may be a reference to the belief that geese were cowardly; it may suggest that Trinculo has a long neck; or it may suggest that, under the cloak, he looks like a tailor's iron, which was called a 'goose'. There is a reference to a tailor in the song Stephano sings when he comes onto the stage
when time was once upon a time. The next few lines deal with beliefs that there was a man in the moon who had a dog that could hide behind a bush
mistress Miranda
anon immediately
sooth truth
kiss thy foot people often kissed the foot of a statue of a saint
puppy-headed stupid
crabs crab apples
pig-nuts possibly groundnuts or truffles
filberts hazelnuts
scamels sea birds
trenchering cleaning the wood on which meat was cut

ACT III

SCENE 1 Near Prospero's dwelling. Miranda and Ferdinand express their love for each other

Unknown to the young couple, Prospero watches while Miranda tries to help Ferdinand in his 'slavery'. She offers to carry some of the logs for him but Ferdinand assures her that his hard work gives him pleasure because he is toiling for her. They confess their love for each other and promise to get married as soon as it is possible. Prospero is delighted that his plan is working and that such deep affection has developed between his daughter and the son of the King of Naples.

Modern readers may react strongly against Prospero's punishment of Ferdinand. It is worth stressing that, for the purposes of dramatic **unity** (see Dramatic Unities), however, Prospero had to show that the young couple's love was deep and abiding, rather than simply physical attraction.

There be some sports ... sets off there are some pains that are worthwhile because they eventually bring great joy and delight
baseness humiliation
quickens brings to life
crabbed annoying, bad-tempered
sore injunction an order that will result in severe punishment if it is not obeyed
baseness ... like executor lowly tasks were never performed by one as fine as he
most busilest even when I am at my busiest
hard at study busy studying. Only the audience knows that Prospero is watching
crack strain to breaking point
Poor worm poor creature
infected madly in love
visitation visit
Miranda a wonder, one to be admired
hest command. Miranda does not willingly break her father's commands
several individual. Ferdinand confesses that he has fallen under the spell of other beautiful women but always found some weakness in them. Only Miranda has been perfect
owed possessed
more that I may call men Miranda does not count Caliban as a man
skilless ignorant
to like of to match
condition position
flesh-fly a fly known to carry germs
blow soil, lay eggs in
kind event favourable outcome

invert … mischief Ferdinand swears that he hopes to miss out on any of the good fortune that lies ahead of him, if he lies about his love
rare unusual and beautiful
die to want die of desire for failing to get what I want
maid both 'servant' and 'virgin'
fellow companion, equal
As bondage e'er of freedom I desire to be bound to you as passionately as a slave desires freedom
a thousand thousand Goodbye a thousand times
book book of magic. Prospero has foreseen the love of the young couple
much business appertaining many things associated with my plans

SCENE 2 Another part of the island. This humorous scene concentrates on Caliban, Stephano and Trinculo and provides interesting insights into the treatment of 'difference' in the seventeenth century

In this scene we meet Caliban, Stephano and Trinculo again. Ariel also takes part in the **action** but he is invisible to the other three. Caliban has been telling Stephano about Prospero and Miranda and encouraging him to kill Prospero and take over control of the island. Trinculo does not like Caliban, and Ariel contributes to the dislike by imitating Trinculo's voice and calling Caliban a liar. Stephano tells Trinculo to leave Caliban alone but Ariel calls him a liar too. Stephano assumes that Trinculo is the culprit and hits him. Trinculo attributes the strange behaviour of Stephano and Caliban to the alcohol they have drunk.

Stephano encourages Caliban to tell them more about Prospero. Caliban reveals that Prospero is helpless without his books and that if Stephano steals them, he will be able to kill Prospero while he is having his afternoon nap. Stephano decides to kill Prospero and take over Miranda and the island. Trinculo decides to accompany Stephano and Caliban, and Ariel rushes off to tell Prospero about the conspiracy.

The attitude to Caliban expressed by Stephano and Trinculo is, by today's standards, politically incorrect and totally unacceptable. It is worth remembering, however, that circuses and sideshows exhibiting so-called 'freaks' were popular even in this century.

bear up and board'em a seafaring expression, here meaning 'drink up'
folly stupidity
brained as intelligent as us
set comic scenes often involve **puns**. This word is used with two different meanings. In line 8 it means 'set in a fixed stare' and in line 9 it means 'placed, positioned'
standard standard bearer, flag carrier. The **punning** continues. When 'no standard' is used later, it means 'not able to stand without support'
list want, please
in case to in the mood to, in the frame of mind to
debosh'd debauched, dissolute
natural fool, idiot
suit request
Marry an oath, originally 'By the Blessed Virgin Mary', meaning 'indeed'
hath cheated me of the island Caliban believes the island was rightfully his and that Prospero had tricked him out of it
supplant knock out
Mum silence. We still use the phrase 'Mum's the word' to mean 'Say nothing'
I'll yield him thee asleep I'll show you how to get at him when he is asleep
pied ninny a multicoloured fool. Trinculo was a jester and would therefore have been wearing a garment of two or more bright colours
patch jester, clown wearing clothing made of coloured patches
quick freshes springs of fresh water
make a stock-fish of thee I'll beat you severely. It was customary to pound fish before it was boiled and dried in order to make it tender
pox ... drinking do Damn this alcohol. This is what happens when we drink
murrain plague
brain him hit him on the head, knock his brains out
paunch him stick a knife in his stomach
wezand windpipe
sot fool, idiot
rootedly firmly, completely
deck decorate, ornament
nonpareil unequalled for beauty
brave brood a fine family. Caliban's **imagery** is taken from the animal kingdom
troll the catch sing the song in parts, loudly and with gusto
while-ere a little while ago, not long ago

flout mock
cout make a fool of
scout sneer at
by the picture of Nobody by an invisible person
take's as thou list take whatever shape you please
airs music. This play, like the island, is 'full of music'
twangling reverberating, plucked
taborer drummer

SCENE 3 Another part of the island. This scene involves a miming masque and provides Alonso with the opportunity to express his remorse for his behaviour towards Prospero

This scene opens with the royal party and the audience discovers that Antonio and Sebastian are still determined to kill Alonso. They plan to do it in the evening, when people are tired and less vigilant. When the group decides to rest, Prospero appears with some spirits and they spread a feast out in front of the hungry men. When they try to eat it, however, Ariel appears in the guise of a harpy and reminds them of their cruelty to Prospero and Miranda. Ariel and the feast then disappear. Alonso is filled with grief for the crime he committed against Prospero, but Antonio and Sebastian are unmoved and decide to fight the spirits of the island.

The introduction of a feast that is spread before them but which they cannot eat is reminiscent of earlier **morality plays** (see Literary Background).

By'r lakin 'By Our Little Lady', a reference to the Blessed Virgin Mary
maze a type of garden where there are so many winding paths that it is not easy to know where one is going. The reference to a maze was topical because the Hampton Court maze was constructed in 1608
forth-rights and meanders both straight and winding paths
attach'd overcome, taken over
frustrate useless, futile
repulse setback
advantage opportunity
throughly thoroughly, completely
keepers guardian angel

drollery puppet show. Sebastian is suggesting that what they now see is as strange as fiction and yet they are witnessing it so it must be true. The banquet interlude in this scene has certain **masque**-like qualities
unicorns mythical horses with a horn in the centre of their foreheads
phoenix mythical bird. When the time came for it to die, it built its own funeral pyre and burnt to death and a new phoenix was believed to emerge from the ashes
certes certainly
monstrous unfamiliar, non-human
muse wonder at
dumb discourse mime
praise in departing Prospero has arranged the apparition and knows what will happen. He is saying 'Don't praise the action until you know how it will end'
Who would believe there were many strange tales brought back to England by travellers. Among them was the 1596 account in Walter Raleigh's writings on Guiana, South America, of a 'nation of people whose heads appear not above their shoulders ... they are reported to have their eyes in their shoulders, and their mouths in the middle of their breasts'
dew-lapped with folds of skin hanging from their throats
Each putter-out of five for one each traveller. In Shakespeare's day, it was common practice for men to deposit a sum of money before going on a long journey. If they did not return or if they did not complete the journey, they forfeited their deposit. If they were successful, however, they got five times the amount of the original sum
harpy a monster that had a woman's face and body but wings and claws like a bird
three men of sin Alonso, Sebastian and Antonio
hath to instrument has complete control over
their proper selves themselves
elements materials. The suggestion is that everything is composed of the four elements – air, earth, fire and water – and that spirits cannot be hurt by objects made from such elements
still-closing if a knife is stuck in the sea, the sea invariably closes round it, showing no trace of a wound
dowle small feather
plume plumage, wing
like likewise, similarly

ACT III SCENE 3 continued

requit it paid you back
wraths ghosts; anger
whose wraths to guard you from ... ensuing if you are to avoid being destroyed by the powers that control your destiny, you must repent and lead pure lives
bravely excellently
a grace it had devouring your performance was both graceful and frightening
observation strange: wonderful care
their several kinds according to their individual talents and natures
knit up completely caught up by
his and mine lov'd darling Miranda is loved by both Ferdinand and Prospero
of it of my sin
bass my trespass call out my sin in a loud, deep voice
plummet a plumb line, a line with a weight on the end of it causing it to sink
bite the spirits affect their moods
ecstasy madness

ACT IV

SCENE 1 In front of Prospero's dwelling. This long scene includes a masque to celebrate the love of the young couple. Caliban's plot to murder Prospero is prevented

Prospero decides that Ferdinand has suffered enough and so he agrees to let him marry Miranda. To celebrate their betrothal he organises a **masque** which is performed by spirits under the direction of Ariel.

The spirits impersonate Greek goddesses. First, Iris, the goddess of the rainbow and messenger of the gods, appears. She introduces Juno, the queen of the gods, and then Ceres, the goddess of fertility and of the harvest. Their speech is poetic and emphasises the joys of marriage. Ferdinand is delighted with the spectacle but there is more to come. Iris calls up the naiads, or spirits of the waters, and they are followed by a group of reapers. The naiads and reapers dance together and their disappearance brings the masque to an end.

The sudden termination of the festivities is caused by Prospero's remembering that Caliban, Stephano and Trinculo are planning to kill him. He apologises to Ferdinand and leaves the young lovers so that he can deal with the three conspirators.

Ariel is called and explains that he has led the three plotters into a stagnant, muddy pool. Ariel is told to bring out some of Prospero's rich garments and hang them on the trees to distract Stephano and Trinculo. Prospero and Ariel then make themselves invisible so that they can watch what happens.

Trinculo, Stephano and Caliban arrive. The first two are annoyed with Caliban because they have lost their wine in the pool. They see the clothes which have been hung up by Ariel and quarrel about who should keep them. Caliban tries to tell them that the garments are merely trash and that their sole concern should be the murder of Prospero. Trinculo and Stephano refuse to listen to Caliban, however, and while they are preparing to carry off the clothes, Prospero and Ariel call up spirits in the shape of hounds which chase the three away from Prospero's cell.

> The potential for tragedy that has hung over this play since the first scene is gradually abating. Love triumphs and 'treachery' is discovered. In theory, Caliban was guilty of insurrection but Shakespeare emphasises that Caliban was motivated by greed less than the more 'civilised' Trinculo and Stephano.

third Prospero is perhaps thinking of the family unit, himself, his dead wife and Miranda. Thus, Miranda is a third of his family. He may also be thinking of all that he prizes: his daughter, his books and his dukedom. In addition, 'thread' was sometimes spelt 'thrid' and pronounced like 'third', so it is possible that Prospero described Miranda as the 'thread' of his life (as part of the reason for his continued existence)
strangely wonderfully, extremely well
against an oracle even if an oracle suggested the opposite
break her virgin-knot have intercourse with Miranda
sanctimonious holy, sacred
aspersion sprinkling with holy water, blessing
Hymen the Greek god of marriage, often depicted carrying a torch
issue children
worser genius bad spirit. This refers to the belief that each person had a good angel to look after their spiritual wellbeing and a bad angel who encouraged the person to perform evil acts
Phoebus in Greek mythology, the god of the sun, depicted as a charioteer, driving the sun around the skies

rabble group, band of people or spirits
vanity illusion, manifestation of power
presently immediately
with a twink very rapidly
mop and mow grimaces, with appropriate facial expressions
conceive understand
good night your vow you will break your promise not to sleep with Miranda
liver the heart was associated with love and the liver with physical desire
corollary an extra one
Iris in Greek mythology, the goddess of the rainbow, messenger of the gods
Ceres in Greek mythology, the goddess of fertility and of the harvest
leas arable land
stover hay
pioned dug
twilled woven
brims edges
cold nymphs chaste maidens
broom-groves gorse-bushes
lass-lorn without the girl he loves
poll-clipt vineyard: vines pruned to promote growth; surrounded by poles
sea-marge shoreline
queen of th'sky: in Roman mythology, Juno is Jupiter's wife and queen
wat'ry arch rainbow, **symbol** of peace between God and humanity
saffron orange to yellow colour, associated with power and peace
bosky wooded
unshrubbed down bare hillside
to estate to give, bestow
Venus or her son in Roman mythology, Venus was the goddess of love and her son was Cupid. Cupid is often depicted as being blind. He caused havoc by making people fall in love with inappropriate partners
dusky Dis the dark coloured god of the underworld. According to Greek legend, Dis, also called Pluto, seized Ceres' daughter, Persephone, and took her back to the underworld to be his wife
scandal'd scandalous, improper
Paphos a town in Cyprus dedicated to Venus; place where the gods met
bed-right permissible love-making sanctioned by marriage
Hymen's torch be lighted the marriage has taken place

hot minion passionate lover. Venus was renowned for her passionate love affairs, including one with Mars, the god of war.
be a boy right out behave just like an ordinary boy
sister Juno and Ceres were both daughters of Saturn
foison rich, abundant harvest
Spring come to you conventional wish equivalent to 'May you never know the rigours of winter. May spring immediately follow autumn'
wonder'd father amazing father to be capable of performing such wonders
naiads spirits of the water in Greek mythology
windring winding and wandering
crisp wave-covered, rippling
temperate chaste and cool
footing dancing
the beast Caliban notice how often the **imagery** surrounding Caliban suggests that he is animal-like or only partly human
avoid go away
works agitates, upsets
distemper'd disturbed, upset
moved sort strange mood
inherit occupy, possess
rack small cloud
rounded rounded off; brought to full circle
with a thought as quickly as you can. This remark is addressed to Ariel
presented performed the part of; acted as master of ceremonies
unback'd colts young horses that have never been ridden
advanc'd lifted up, raised
goss: gorse
o'erstunk their feet smelt worse than their feet
trumpery rich-looking clothes
for stale as a decoy
devil Prospero is referring to Caliban and arguing that, no matter how kindly he is treated, he will behave badly. The audience and the readers will make their own decisions about the 'pains' that Prospero took with Caliban
Nurture education, training. The argument here centres on the relative values of nature (inherited characteristics) and nurture (training) in a person's development

blind mole this small animal was believed to be blind but to have acute hearing
played the Jack with us made fools of us, tricked us
hoodwink this mischance make up for this mistake
o'er ears overheard; knocked head over heels
good mischief an action that may appear bad but has good results
trash worthless. Caliban knows the difference between *real* and *apparent* value
frippery a shop that sold old clothes
dropsy illness where fluids gather in the body
luggage useless trappings
make us strange stuff turn us into strange shapes
line punning on meanings, including 'clothes line', the 'equator' and 'lime tree'
lose your hair when sailors crossed the 'line' (the equator), some shaved their heads to avoid catching a fever
by line and level accurately, systematically
an't like if it please
pass of pate witty remark
lime birdlime, which was very sticky
barnacles geese
Mountain, Silver, Fury, Tyrant the names of the hunting dogs
dry convulsions tremors thought to be caused by a lack of fluid in the joints
pinch-spotted black and blue with bruises
cat o' mountain leopard

ACT V

SCENE 1 In front of Prospero's dwelling. The play ends with hope for the future, with forgiveness for earlier wrong, with freedom for Ariel, and with Caliban again in control of his island

Prospero's plans are now reaching fulfilment, so he sends Ariel to bring the royal party to his cell. Alonso, Sebastian and Antonio have been kept in a distracted state by one of Prospero's spells. Prospero reveals himself to the party, rebukes Alonso, Antonio and Sebastian for the evil they have done, then forgives them all and thanks Gonzalo for his kindness. Alonso still believes that his son is dead but Prospero shows him the young couple playing chess. Alonso rejoices in their happiness and adds his blessing to their proposed marriage.

Ariel next brings in the ship's captain and boatswain and they tell the company that the ship is seaworthy and ready for the journey back to Italy.

Finally, Ariel leads in Trinculo, Stephano and Caliban. The jester and the butler are reprimanded by Alonso. Caliban admits that he was foolish to regard Stephano as a god and he promises 'I'll be wise hereafter / And seek for grace' (V.1.294–5).

Prospero agrees to resume his dukedom in Milan but first he invites the royal party to spend the night in his cell and listen to the story of the last twelve years. In keeping with his promise, he releases Ariel.

All the **subplots** are integrated; tragedy has been averted; love and reconciliation are stressed. The audience might subsequently wonder why Antonio and Sebastian are treated so much more leniently than Caliban was, but the play ends on a note of hope.

crack not are proving adequate
On the sixth hour about six o'clock
gave in charge ordered, commanded
line-grove small wood of lime trees
weather-fends protects your cell from bad weather
till your release until you release them
eaves of reeds thatched roofs
relish feel
kindlier more naturally and more generously
high wrongs serious offences
the rarer action ... in vengeance it is better to forgive than to seek revenge
ebbing Neptune the sea going out
fly him hurry away from him
demi-puppets small, doll-like fairies
green sour ringlets fairy rings of toadstools in the grass. Toadstools cannot be eaten because they are poisonous or 'sour'
midnight mushrooms it was thought that fairies made mushrooms at night
weak masters beings with limited powers
azur'd vault blue sky

Jove's stout oak Jove, king of the gods in Roman mythology, was also the god of thunder. The oak, which is a very strong tree, was under Jove's protection
graves ... oped Prospero is taking to himself powers greater than those possessed by the gods of mythology
airy charm musical spell
I'll break my staff ... I'll drown my books Prospero renounces his magical powers by casting aside the symbols of this art. There is more than an echo here of Christopher Marlowe's play, *Doctor Faustus* (1592). In it, Faustus exchanged his soul for twenty-four years of knowledge and power. When Lucifer came to collect his soul, Faustus pleaded 'Ugly hell, gape not! Lucifer! / I'll burn my books!' (*Doctor Faustus*, Act V, Scene 2)
boiled over-excited
spell-stopped completely under the influence of my spell
ev'n sociable to fully in sympathy with
Fall let fall, drop
mantle cloak, cover, shield
thy graces Home your services to the full
furtherer accessory
remorse and nature pity and natural feelings
inward pinches pangs of conscience
unnatural evil and counter to the laws of God and nature. The Stuart kings believed firmly in the doctrine of 'the divine right of kings', according to which kings owed their position to God. To attack a king, therefore, was to go against the will of God
swell grow, rise as the sea rises
reasonable shore shore of reason, the mind
discase me remove my outer garment
sometime Milan formerly Duke of Milan
enforce them bring them here by force, if necessary
fearful country island which can inspire fear in its inhabitants
for more assurance in order to make you more aware
enchanted trifle to abuse magic trick meant to deceive
amends grows less acute
crave require, ask for and receive
An if this be at all if this is really true and not just a trick
Thy dukedom I resign I hand back your dukedom to you
my wrongs my sins

subtleties magic flavour
justify cause you to be seen as, prove
woe sorry
as late and as recent
dear loss serious loss
I perceive these lords Prospero suggests that the lords have been so amazed by all that has happened that they can no longer believe the evidence of their eyes or ears
do ... admire wonder at, are astonished
devour their reason their reason is overcome by their amazement
do offices provide evidence
justled knocked out of
abroad elsewhere on the island
play me false are not playing fairly
yes, for a score of kingdoms Miranda claims that Ferdinand might argue about the rights and wrongs of the game, but she would always think that what he did was acceptable
vision illusion
eld'st longest
renown reports, rumours
heaviness sadness, sorrow
inly inwardly
still always
Now blasphemy Gonzalo suggests that the boatswain's swearing on board ship was the cause of their shipwreck and he notices that the boatswain does not swear now that he is ashore
gave out split reported to be wrecked
tight and yare not leaking and ready for a journey
tricksy agile, resourceful
several different, distinct
on a trice in a moment
diligent hardworking, conscientious spirit
was ever conduct of ever caused
infest your mind with beating worry yourself by trying to understand
shortly single soon and in private
resolve you explain everything to you
coragio (Italian) courage

true spies reliable witnesses, that is, good eyes
Setebos Caliban's mother's god. Caliban has never given up his own gods
badges servants often wore a uniform or emblems to indicate their employer
deal in her command use the moon's powers against the moon's will
thing of darkness Prospero may be referring to Caliban's evil nature, to his dark skin or to the fact that he was conceived in the dark
reeling ripe extremely drunk
gilded 'em made them drunk
in a pickle in trouble; in a liquid which is a preservative
fly-blowing flies which contaminate meat. Trinculo need not fear contamination because he has been pickled
I am not Stephano, but a cramp I have cramps all over my body
waste use up, spend
accidents incidents
chick dear one

EPILOGUE

Prospero addresses the audience. He assures them that he has laid aside his magical powers, has forgiven his enemies and has been given back his dukedom. All he needs now is to be set free from the spell cast on him by the audience and this can be done by their applause.

overthrown brought to an end
confined by you held by you, the audience
With the help of your good hands by applauding. It was not unusual to have a main character address the audience at the end of the play and it is appropriate that, at the end of a play dealing with magic, Prospero should ask the audience to release him from their spell by applauding the play
want lack

PART THREE

CRITICAL APPROACHES

CHARACTER EVALUATION

Shakespeare's characters are usually subtly drawn. Like living human beings, they are rarely completely good or completely bad, and can show different sides of their nature depending on the people they are with or the circumstances in which they find themselves. In *The Tempest*, however, it has been suggested that the main characters are at one and the same time naturalistic and representational. At one level, the four main characters on the island may be said to represent different attributes of humanity: instinct – Caliban; love – Miranda; spirit – Ariel; and power – Prospero.

But such a generalisation should be challenged and discussed rather than simply accepted. It does, however, seem true that in his last plays, *Pericles*, *The Winter's Tale* and *The Tempest*, Shakespeare is more interested in dealing with human weaknesses and human destiny than in delineating highly idiosyncratic characters.

PROSPERO

Prospero plays the most significant role in the play in that he is on the stage longer than any other character and he controls the fate of all the others on the island. You might like to consider whether he uses his powers wisely and humanely or selfishly.

He lost his dukedom because he failed to recognise his brother's ambition and because he neglected his first duty, the governing of Milan. As he himself tells Miranda:

> The government I cast upon my brother,
> And to my state grew stranger, being transported
> And rapt in secret studies. (I.2.75–7)

His treatment by his brother, Antonio, has taught him not to trust appearances. It may look as if Ferdinand loves Miranda but Prospero is determined to test the strength of this love: 'They are both in either's pow'rs: but this swift business / I must uneasy make, lest too light winning / Make the prize light (I.2.453–5).

You might ask yourself if Prospero is as affectionate and caring as he suggests. For example, he tells Miranda that 'I have done nothing but in care of thee; / Of thee, my dear one; thee, my daughter' (I.2.16–17) although it was his behaviour that caused Miranda's fate in the first place. His attitude towards others should also be considered. He seems to love Ariel: 'Do you love me master? / Dearly, my delicate Ariel' (IV.1.48–9), yet he can behave cruelly to him: '... malignant thing! Hast thou forgot / The foul witch Sycorax, who with age and envy / Was grown into a hoop? has thou forgot her?' (I.2 257–9). Prospero also shows love for and gratitude towards Gonzalo, describing him as 'A noble Neapolitan, Gonzalo' (I.2.161) and later, when he meets Gonzalo face to face, he is moved to tears by the old man's goodness: 'Holy Gonzalo, honourable man, / Mine eyes, ev'n sociable to the show of shine, / Fall fellowly drops' (V.1.62–6). Prospero remembers the evil of Alonso, Antonio and Sebastian but forgives them:

> Though with their high wrongs I am struck to th' quick,
> Yet with my nobler reason 'gainst my fury
> Do I take part: the rarer action is
> In virtue than in vengeance: they being penitent,
> The sole drift of my purpose doth extend
> Not a frown further. (V.1.25–30)

His harshness towards Caliban must rate as Prospero's greatest weakness. It is true that Caliban tried to rape Miranda: 'thou didst seek to violate / The honour of my child' (I.2.349–50), but the language he uses to Caliban seems unnecessarily severe: 'Thou most lying slave, / Whom stripes may move, not kindness! I have us'd, / Filth as thou art, with human care' (I.2.346–8) and it is vindictive to plague Caliban with arthritis:

> Hag-seed, hence!
> Fetch us in fuel; and be quick, thou'rt best,
> To answer other business. Shrug'st thou, malice?
> If thou neglect'st, or dost unwillingly
> What I command, I'll rack thee with old cramps,
> Fill all thy bones with aches, make thee roar,
> That beasts shall tremble at thy din. (I 2.367–73)

Caliban

Caliban is, to a modern audience, one of the most interesting and sympathetic characters in thc play. He is described in the **Folio** edition of *The Tempest* as 'a salvage and deformed slave'. The word 'salvage' is an earlier form of modern 'savage' but in Shakespeare's day it meant 'wild and uncivilised' rather than 'cruel or bestial'. Most people in England believed that uncivilised people were below their civilised counterparts in the hierarchy that had God at its apex and inanimate nature at its base. However, some were beginning to question this assumption and there is evidence in the play that Shakespeare believed that the corruption in so-called 'civilised' society was more abhorrent than any natural behaviour.

Caliban's name may be an anagram of 'cannibal', often spelt with one 'n' in Shakespeare's day, or it may derive from 'Cariban' since people in England were familiar with stories about Carib Indians. Caliban's deformity is never exactly specified. He is insultingly referred to as a 'tortoise' (I.2.318), a 'fish' (II.2.25) and a 'beast' (IV.1.140) and in the final act Prospero describes him as 'This misshapen knave' (V.1.268) and as one who is 'as disproportion'd in his manners' (V.1.290–1).

Much of what we know about his parentage and background comes from Prospero who was prejudiced: 'Thou poisonous slave, got by the devil himself / Upon thy wicked dam' (I.2.321–2). Caliban is about twenty-four and had lived on the island for twelve years before the arrival of Prospero and Miranda. At first, Caliban says, he and Prospero were friends:

> When thou cam'st first
> Thou strok'st me, and made much of me; wouldst give me
> Water with berries in't; and teach me how
> To name the bigger light, and how the less,
> That burn by day and night: and then I lov'd thee,
> And show'd thee all the qualities o' th' isle,
> The fresh springs, brine-pits, barren place and fertile. (I 2.334–40)

Caliban does not refute Prospero's claim 'thou didst seek to violate / The honour of my child' (I.2.349–50). Rather, he regrets his lack of success: 'would 't had been done! / Thou didst prevent me; I had peopled else / This isle with Calibans' (I.2 351–3). Even though Caliban has been enslaved by Prospero, he risks punishment by using the 'thou' form, normally only acceptable to inferiors or intimate equals, and his service is grudging because he regards Prospero as a usurper: 'This island's mine, / Which thou tak'st from me' (I.2.332–3). He plots with Stephano and Trinculo to kill Prospero:

> Why, as I told thee, 'tis a custom with him
> I' th' afternoon to sleep: there thou mayst brain him,
> Having first seiz'd his books; or with a log
> Batter his skull, or paunch him with a stake,
> Or cut his wezand with thy knife. (II.2.86–9)

Caliban shows considerable intelligence. He has learnt Prospero's language: 'You taught me language; and my profit on't / Is, I know how to curse' (I.2.365–6) and is fully aware of the futility of arguing with one who has more power than he has: 'I must obey: his Art is of such pow'r, / It would control my dam's god, Setebos, / And make a vassal of him' (I.2.374–6). Caliban has a better set of values than Stephano and Trinculo. They are distracted from their plan by their greed for Prospero's rich garments. Only Caliban realises that such finery is unimportant: 'Leave it alone, thou fool, it is but trash' (IV.1.224).

Caliban is sensitive to beauty and is given some of the most poetic lines in the play:

> the isle is full of noises,
> Sounds and sweet airs, that give delight, and hurt not.
> Sometimes a thousand twangling instruments
> Will hum about mine ears; and sometime voices,
> That, if I then had wak'd after long sleep,
> Will make me sleep again: and then, in dreaming,
> The clouds methought would open, and show riches
> Ready to drop upon me; that, when I wak'd, I cried to dream again.
> (III.2.133–41)

Caliban's motive for murder is less ignoble than that of Antonio and Sebastian. They plan to kill Alonso to gain his power and wealth. Caliban merely wants the return of 'his' island. You might like to think about whether Caliban's 'conversion' – 'I'll be wise hereafter, / And seek for grace' (V.1.295–6) – is likely or whether it is the result of tidying up all the strands in the **plot**

ARIEL

As his name implies, Ariel is a spirit of the air, swift and delicate, ethereal and occasionally mischievous. Ariel is obedient to Prospero and although he longs for his freedom he seems to take pleasure in his work:

> All hail, great master! grave sir, hail! I come
> To answer thy best pleasure; be't to fly.
> To swim, to dive into the fire, to ride
> On the curl'd clouds, to thy strong bidding task. (I.2.189–93)

He certainly deserves the freedom he asks for (I.2.245) because, as he reminds Prospero, he has never lied or cheated: 'Remember I have done thee worthy service: / Told thee no lies, made no mistakings, serv'd / Without grudge or grumblings' (I.2.247–9). It is interesting to contrast the terms of endearment applied to Ariel, 'my dainty Ariel', 'my bird', 'my Ariel, chick' with the terms of opprobrium hurled at Caliban.

Although not human, he is moved to pity by the plight of the royal party:

> ARIEL: Your charm so strongly works 'em,
> That if you now beheld them, your affections would become tender.
>
> PROSPERO: Dost thou think so, spirit?
>
> ARIEL: Mine would, sir, were I human (V.1.17 –20)

One of Ariel's key roles in *The Tempest* is to provide music. His melodies are heard throughout the island and they can control the actions of the characters. Caliban is frequently lulled by airs: 'that give delight' (III.2.134) and Ferdinand is lured to his meeting with Miranda by Ariel's music. You may agree that Ariel's nature excites the audience's admiration and that his music gives pleasure, but does his character lack the depth and complexity of Caliban's?

MIRANDA

Miranda is the only woman in the play. Her name is the equivalent of 'the wonderful one' or 'the one who causes admiration' and her name is symbolic of her beauty, innocence and modesty. When the play opens

Miranda is almost fifteen and, for the previous twelve years, she has lived on the island and has known only Prospero and Caliban. All who know Miranda are impressed by her beauty. Ferdinand thinks she is so lovely that she must be a goddess: 'Most sure the goddess / On whom these airs attend!' (I.2.424–5).

Miranda feels sympathy for the suffering of others. Indeed, the first words attributed to her in the play are an expression of her concern for those involved in the shipwreck:

> If by your Art, my dearest father, you have
> Put the wild waters in this roar, allay them.
> The sky, it seems, would pour down stinking pitch,
> But that the sea, mounting to th' welkin's cheek,
> Dashes the fire out. O, I have suffered
> With those that I saw suffer! (I.2.1–6)

She shows sympathy for everyone in pain except Caliban, whom she dislikes because he attempted to rape her and she tries to avoid seeing him: 'Tis a villain, sir, / I do not love to look on' (I.2.310–12).

Miranda falls in love at first sight and she has the simplicity and forthrightness to express her love openly. Shortly after meeting Ferdinand she tells him: 'I am your wife if you will marry me; / If not, I'll die your maid' (III.1.83–4). The same quality of directness is shown in her open admiration of the attractive men in the courtly party: 'How many goodly creatures are there here! / How beauteous mankind is! O brave new world, / That has such people in't!' (V.1.181–3). Yet, in spite of the immediacy of Miranda's love for Ferdinand, it seems to be a love that will endure and it is certainly a generous love. When Miranda sees Ferdinand carrying logs, she is eager to share his labour and tells him: 'If you'll sit down, I'll bear your logs the while: pray give me that; / I'll carry it to the pile' (III.1.23–5).

Miranda is beautiful, sympathetic, a character without blemish or artifice. You can judge for yourself whether such an idealisation of womanhood makes a heroine that we can identify with.

FERDINAND

Ferdinand is handsome, courageous and honourable. His good looks impress Miranda so much that she thinks he is a spirit, albeit a fine looking one: 'I might call him / A thing divine; for nothing natural / I ever saw so noble' (I.2.420–2). His courage in adversity is suggested by Francisco, who saw him jump into the sea and swim towards the island: 'I saw him beat the surges under him, / And ride upon their backs; he trod the water, / Whose enmity he flung aside' (II.1.110–12) and he bravely attempts to withstand imprisonment by Prospero: 'I will resist such entertainment till / Mine enemy has more pow'r' (I.2.468–9).

Ferdinand is a loving son. He grieves for the father he believes he has lost and describes himself as one: 'Who with mine eyes, never since at ebb, beheld / The King my father wrack'd' (I.2.438–9). His love for Miranda is instantaneous but sincere and profound. He is willing to give up his throne and his country for her: 'Let me live here ever; / So rare a wonder'd father and a wise / Makes this place Paradise' (IV.1.122–4). His love is gentle and protective. He is touched when Miranda offers to share his labour but will not let her suffer on his behalf:

> No, precious creature;
> I had rather crack my sinews, break my back,
> Than you should such dishonour undergo,
> While I sit lazy by. (III.1.25–8)

ALONSO

Alonso, the King of Naples, has sinned in the past, but he shows himself to be capable of remorse and to have a keen desire to repent. His crime against Prospero was inspired by Antonio, but he showed weakness in succumbing to Antonio's temptation and cruelty in allowing Prospero and Miranda to be 'Expos'd unto the sea' (III.3.71).

Alonso is shown to have a number of redeeming qualities. He loves his son deeply and is grieved by his disappearance: 'O thou mine heir / Of Naples and of Milan, what strange fish / Hath made his meal on thee?' (II.1.107–9). So, in spite of fatigue, he searches the island for him: 'let's make further search / For my poor son' (II.1.318–9). Alonso is capable of inspiring devotion in his followers. Gonzalo loves him and defends him against Sebastian's criticism:

> My lord Sebastian,
> The truth thou speak doth lack some gentleness,

> And time to speak it in: you rub the sore,
> When you should bring the plaster. (II.1.131–4)

When Alonso is condemned by Ariel for his crimes against Prospero and Miranda, his conscience is pricked to such an extent that he thinks of committing suicide:

> O, it is monstrous, monstrous!
> Methought the billows spoke and told me of it
> The winds did sing it to me, and the thunder,
> That deep and dreadful organ-pipe, pronounced
> The name of Prosper: it did bass my trespass.
> Therefore my son i' the ooze is bedded, and
> I'll seek him deeper than e'er plummet sounded
> And with him there lie mudded. (III.3.95–102)

You might like to ask yourself if there is any justice in the claims made by Antonio and Sebastian (II.1.118ff) that Alonso had sacrificed his daughter for the sake of a profitable alliance.

GONZALO

Gonzalo is described by Prospero as a 'noble Neapolitan' (I.2.161). He is an old man who is well-intentioned and talkative. You might like to compare him with Polonius in *Hamlet*, a character that, according to tradition, Shakespeare himself played. Antonio mocks the old man's garrulity (II.1.258–60), claiming that his 'prating' is longwinded and of no value. His statements provide a commentary on the various incidents in the **plot**, from the shipwreck to the discovery of Ferdinand and Miranda. His remarks are usually optimistic and he seems cheerful even in the midst of disaster. In the first scene of the play, for example, he assures the others that they will not drown because the boatswain has the appearance of a man who will hang: 'I have great comfort from this fellow: methinks he hath no drowning mark upon him; his complexion is perfect gallows' (I.1.28–30).

Gonzalo has been loyal to Alonso for at least twelve years. It is worth remembering that he is a Neapolitan and thus a subject of Alonso and not of Prospero. His sense of justice, however, persuaded him to treat Prospero and Miranda with kindness and so he provided them with: 'Rich garments, linens, stuffs, and necessaries' (I.2.164) as well as with food, water and books from Prospero's library. His continued loyalty to Alonso is shown in his reproach to Sebastian: 'My lord Sebastian, / The truth you speak doth lack some gentleness' (II.1.132–3). Prospero praises the old man's loyalty and perhaps sums up the audience's reaction to a likeable, loyal, talkative and cheerful nobleman: 'O good Gonzalo, / My true preserver, and a loyal sir / To him thou follow'st' (V.1.68–70).

Antonio

Antonio is Prospero's brother. Prospero loved and trusted him but Antonio proved false: 'My brother, and thy uncle, call'd Antonio, / … he whom next thyself / Of all the world I lov'd' (I.2.66–70). Antonio is a pragmatist. He made an arrangement with Alonso, King of Naples, to deprive Prospero of his dukedom and paid a yearly levy to the king. According to Prospero, Antonio would have killed Miranda and himself but he was afraid the people would not tolerate such an action since 'So dear the love my people bore me' (I.2.141).

Antonio seems to have lived well since Prospero's banishment and he was on sufficiently good terms with the king to be invited to the wedding of Alonso's daughter in Tunis. He does not seem to have suffered from a guilty conscience for his action towards Prospero. When Sebastian suggests that his conscience may have pricked him he replies: 'if't were a kibe, / 'Twould put me to my slipper: but I feel not / This deity in my bosom' (II.1.271–3). Antonio tempts Sebastian to kill his brother, Alonso, and actually offers to perform the action:

> Here lies your brother,
> No better than the earth he lies upon,
> If he were that which now he's like, that's dead;
> Whom I, with this obedient steel, three inches of it
> Can lay to bed for ever; (II.1.275–9)

He knows human nature well and suggests that the majority of men will follow the person who has the power, irrespective of how he got it. Nevertheless, he is aware that Gonzalo is sincerely loyal to Alonso and so advises Sebastian to kill him.

Antonio has a sense of humour, as is shown in his witty exchanges with Sebastian in the first part of Act II, Scene 1, yet it is a cruel sense of humour, taking pleasure in mocking the talkativeness of an old man. In spite of all his weaknesses, however, Antonio has courage. He is as disturbed as the others by the disappearance of the banquet in Act III, Scene 3, and as frightened as they are by Ariel's apparition, and yet he is prepared to follow Sebastian and fight the spirits (III.3.102–3).

Antonio shows no sign whatsoever of having repented any of his crimes and yet he is included in Prospero's general absolution:

> For you, most wicked sir, whom to call brother
> Would even infect my mouth, I do forgive
> Thy rankest faults, all of them; and require
> My dukedom of thee, which perforce, I know,
> Thou must restore. (V.1.130–4)

You might like to think about the facts that Antonio neither thanks Prospero for his forgiveness nor comments on the loss of the dukedom. Indeed, he does not utter more than a few words for the rest of the play. Perhaps he had received the hardest punishment an ambitious man could receive, the loss of the temporal power he had fought so hard to attain.

SEBASTIAN

Sebastian is Alonso's brother and his friendship with Antonio suggests the nature of his character. Like Antonio, he mocks Gonzalo (II.1.11–100) and an indication of the ungenerous nature of such repartee is the fact that the passage is in prose not verse.

Sebastian seems to have been involved in Prospero's banishment though his exact role is not indicated. Ariel criticises him in the same terms that he applies to Alonso and Antonio: 'You are three men of sin' (III.3.53) and 'you three / From Milan did supplant good Prospero' (III.3.69–70). Sebastian immediately succumbs to Antonio's temptation to kill Alonso, promising Antonio a reward for his services:

> Thy case, dear friend,
> Shall be my precedent; as thou got'st Milan,
> I'll come by Naples. Draw thy sword: one stroke
> Shall free thee from the tribute which thou payest;
> And I the King shall love thee. (II.1.285–9)

Sebastian has courage. When Ariel and his spirits disappear, he is prepared to follow them and fight them one by one: 'But one fiend at a time, I'll fight their legions o'er' (III.3.102–3). Like Antonio, he shows little sign of repentance and yet is included in Prospero's forgiveness. He also seems more willing to accept the fact that his plot has failed and to make the best of the situation. He rejoices (or appears to rejoice?) in Ferdinand's discovery 'A most high miracle!' (V.1.177) and joins in the amused criticism of Stephano. Shakespeare leaves us in no doubt that Sebastian is an evil man but perhaps his evil may be said to be triggered by Antonio rather than to come from any obvious personal predisposition towards sinfulness.

STEPHANO AND TRINCULO

Stephano and Trinculo play minor roles but they provide much of the humour of the play and act as a contrast to the courtly characters, on one side, and to Caliban, on the other.

RECURRING THEMES

There are many recurrent themes in *The Tempest*, the most marked of which are the following. Some of the comments here are posed as questions to allow you to make up your own mind about the significance of the theme:

GOD AND HUMANITY: Is the play an **allegory**? Does Prospero represent God? Was the usurping of Prospero by his brother a recasting of the Cain and Abel story or indeed the usurping of Richard III's throne by Henry VII, the grandfather of Elizabeth I?

LOVE: How many kinds of love do we find? parent to child? woman to man? brother to brother? master to 'slave'? Why are they introduced?

MAGIC: Is it ever used benignly? (Think about Sycorax's imprisonment of Ariel and Prospero's enslavement of Caliban and insistence on service from Ariel.) You might like to think about the fact that the **plot** of *The Tempest* is unlike many of Shakespeare's other plays in that it depends almost entirely on the use of supernatural powers. In *Macbeth*, for example, the witches may have an influence on the hero's behaviour but he has free will and is thus capable of determining his own actions. This is not true of *The Tempest*, however, where the destiny of everyone from Prospero to Ariel, from Alonso to Caliban, is decided by supernatural intervention rather than by their characters or their actions. It is, of course, important to stress that, in Shakespeare's time, there was widespread belief in the power of magic. Part of this belief was the result of living in a harsh society where education was limited to the few and where there often seemed no natural explanation for events. An additional point worthy of some consideration is that certain places were associated with magic: wells, cross-roads, hawthorn groves. In *The Tempest*, the entire island has strong associations with the supernatural. Caliban's mother, Sycorax, a renowned witch, was banished there; Ariel and the other spirits belong on the island; Prospero's magical powers seem to have developed only after he reached it and they are given up before he leaves. It is as if the island is enchanted. As Caliban says:

> the isle is full of noises,
> Sounds and sweet airs, that give delight, and hurt not.
> Sometimes a thousand twangling instruments
> Will hum about mine ears; and sometime voices,
> That, if I then had wak'd after long sleep,
> Will make me sleep again: and then, in dreaming,
> The clouds methought would open, and show riches
> Ready to drop upon me; that, when I wak'd,
> I cried to dream again. (III.2.133–41)

NATURE AND NURTURE: Could we not say that Prospero's attempt to nurture Caliban had failed because the nurture was meant to control him and not to free him? Is it true that Caliban is the only character who truly understands and loves nature, as it is represented on the island?

NEW WORLD AND OLD WORLD: Is the 'new' world of the island preferable to the 'old' world of Naples? Why does Miranda refer to the latter as 'O brave new world!'? (You might like to compare the island in *The Tempest* with the theme of the forest in *As You Like It*.)

POWER: Are we shown that its use by Prospero does not give him absolute satisfaction and that it does not actually change the nature of either Caliban or Ariel? What are we shown about the desire for power as illustrated by Antonio and Sebastian, at one level, and Stephano and Trinculo at another?

Reconciliation: Is Prospero truly reconciled to life on the island? Why not? Is he fully reconciled to his brother? More to the point, perhaps, is Antonio reconciled to Prospero or will he want to be Duke of Milan again? Is Caliban reconciled to the morality of Prospero in spite of his final words?

The tempest: You might like to think about the relevance of the theme of the tempest, a theme that has had, for millennia, spiritual as well as physical significance. The Christian churches frequently use readings associated with storms, often combining, for example, a reading from the book of Job, with a psalm and the story of Christ calming the waters.

Job, 38:1, 8–11, 25 and 35

1 Then the Lord answered Job out of the whirlwind and said: …

8 Or who shut up the sea with doors, when it brake forth, as if it had issued out of the womb?

9 When I made the cloud the garment thereof, and thick darkness a swaddlingband for it,

10 And brake up for it my decreed place, and set bars and doors,

11 And said, Hitherto shalt thou come, but no further: and here shalt thy proud waves be stayed?

25 Who hath divided a watercourse for the overflowing of waters, or a way for the lightning of thunder;

35 Canst thou send lightnings, that they may go, and say unto thee, Here we are?

Psalm, 107 (106)

23 They that go down to the sea in ships, that do business in great waters;

24 These see the works of the Lord, and his wonders in the deep.

25 For he commandeth, and raiseth the stormy wind, which lifteth up the waves thereof.

28 Then they cry unto the Lord in their trouble, and he bringeth them out of their distresses.

29 He maketh the storm a calm, so that the waves thereof are still.

Mark, 4: 37 and 39 (Résumé: Christ stilleth the tempest)

> 37 And there arose a great storm of wind, and the waves beat into the ship, so that it was now full.
>
> 39 And he arose, and rebuked the wind, and said unto the sea, Peace, be still. And the wind ceased, and there was a great calm.

Finally, we should point out how often, in his plays, Shakespeare uses a play within a play. In *The Tempest*, we have the **masque** and the masque-like sequence of the banquet; in a play such as *Hamlet*, we have the play that was intended to prove Claudius's guilt.

THE HANDLING OF TIME

The treatment of time causes two major problems in *The Tempest*. Because Shakespeare adheres to the classical **unities** (see Dramatic Unities), much of the information required by the audience has to be provided by narration rather than by action. Thus, most of the history of Antonio's treachery to his brother is provided in Prospero's long account in Act I, Scene 2 under the pretext of telling Miranda about her past. It is undoubtedly a mark of Shakespeare's skill that he can incorporate so much background information into a reasonably naturalistic scene. Even then, he breaks it up for both Miranda and the audience by bringing in Ariel with his account of the shipwreck.

The second temporal problem relates to the compression of events. In the space of approximately four hours, the audience is asked to 'believe' that,

- A shipwreck has occurred
- Ferdinand meets and falls in love with Miranda, and has the time to carry logs and convince Prospero that his feelings for Miranda are genuine
- Antonio and Sebastian plot the murder of Alonso
- Caliban, Trinculo and Stephano plot the murder of Prospero
- Alonso undergoes a conversion and repents for his crime against Prospero
- A marriage is arranged
- The plotters are forgiven
- Ariel is freed and Caliban left in control of his island
- The ship is found to be seaworthy and the party prepares to leave the island

In your analysis of the play, you must ask yourself if the speed with which the audience is carried along makes us overlook such temporal improbabilities. Is the time scheme any more unlikely in *The Tempest* than in *Othello* or *The Winter's Tale*? When we go to the theatre, are we not conditioned to accept the constraints of time imposed by the writer? Do we not, in Samuel Taylor Coleridge's phrase, 'willingly suspend our disbelief'?

LANGUAGE AND STYLE

Every living language changes. Differences in pronunciation and in linguistic preferences are often apparent even in the speech of parents and their children, so it is not surprising that the language of Shakespeare's plays should be markedly different from the English we use almost four centuries later. In the sixteenth century, the English language was only beginning to be used by creative writers. Previously, Latin and French had been considered more suitable for literary expression than English and consequently the English language had not been as fully developed as it later became.

The main differences between Shakespearean and modern English can, for convenience, be considered under such categories as mobility of word classes, vocabulary loss, verb forms, pronouns, prepositions, multiple negation and spelling and punctuation.

MOBILITY OF WORD CLASSES

Adjectives, nouns and verbs were less rigidly confined to their specific classes in Shakespeare's day. Adjectives were often used as adverbs. In V.1.309, Prospero describes the lovers as 'our dear belov'd' where modern standard usage would require 'our dearly beloved'. Adjectives could also be used as nouns. In I.2.329, Prospero speaks of 'that vast of night' where today we would prefer 'vastness' or perhaps 'vast abyss'. Nouns were often used as verbs. In I.2.344, Caliban complains 'and here you sty me' where the noun 'sty' is used as if it were a verb with the meaning of 'keep me in a filthy place'. Verbs were also, on occasion, used as nouns. In I.2.69, for example, when Prospero explains that he had neglected his prime duty by entrusting to his brother, Antonio, 'The manage of my state', the verb 'manage' is used in a context where we would today need 'management'.

CHANGES IN WORD MEANING

Words change their meanings as time passes and so many words used by Shakespeare have different values today. Such semantic changes can be illustrated by the following examples:

Word	Meaning in play	Current meaning	Reference
admire	wonder at	look at with pleasure	V.1.154
complexion	total outward appearance	natural facial colouring	I.1.29
engine	instrument of war	machine	II.1.157

VOCABULARY LOSS

One of the difficulties faced by a member of a contemporary audience is the fact that many of the words used by the playwright are no longer current in modern English. For example:

Word	Meaning in *The Tempest*	Reference
bombard	a vessel used for carrying liquids	II.2.21
bootless	useless, without value	I.2.35
bosky	covered and shaded by trees	IV.1.82
chough	jackdaw	II.1.261
doit	small coin worth about a halfpenny	II.2.32

VERB FORMS

Shakespearean verb forms differ from modern usage in three main ways. First, questions and negatives could be formed without using 'do' or 'did'. Thus, in II.2.311 Alonso asks Gonzalo 'Heard you this, Gonzalo?' where today one would have to say 'Did you hear this, Gonzalo?' Similarly, in II.1.272 Antonio says 'but I feel not / This deity in my bosom', using a construction that would be considered ungrammatical in modern English. We must add, however, that Shakespeare often formed questions and negatives as we do today. In I.1.13, for example, the boatswain asks 'Do you not hear him?' and in I.2.40, Prospero tells Miranda 'I do not think thou canst'. Summing up, we can say that whereas Shakespeare could use both the A and B forms shown below, modern English permits only the B structures.

A	B
Like you it?	Do you like it?
I like it not	I do not like it
Liked you it?	Did you like it?
I liked it not	I did not like it

Secondly, some past tense forms are used which would be ungrammatical today. Among the many examples to be found are the following:

Form in *The Tempest*	Current form	Reference
blessedly holp hither	blessedly helped here	I.2.63
Hast thou forgot …	Have you forgotten …	I.2.257
I have broke your hest	I have broken your command	III.1.37
my enemies are all knit up	My enemies are all knitted up	III.3.89
Fairly spoke	Fairly spoken	IV. 1.31

Thirdly, archaic forms of the verb occur with the pronoun 'thou' and, on occasion, with the pronouns 'he', 'she' and 'it', for example, 'Thou didst smile' (I.2.153) and 'he hath lost his fellows' (I.2.418).

PRONOUNS

Shakespeare's pronoun usage differs to some extent from our own. There was a certain amount of choice in the use of second person pronouns in Elizabethan English. *You* had to be used:

- When addressing more than one person and so the boatswain uses it when rebuking the royal party 'Do you not hear him? You mar our labour: keep your cabins' (I.1.13–14).
- When a speaker wished to indicate respect. Thus Miranda and Ferdinand show their mutual respect by addressing each other as 'you':

> MIRANDA: Do you love me?
>
> FERDINAND: O heaven, O earth, bear witness to this sound,
> And crown what I profess with kind event,
> If I speak true! if hollowly, invert
> What best is boded me to mischief! I,
> Beyond all limit of what else i' th' world,
> Do love, prize, honour you. (III.1.67–73)

- Superiors often used *thou* to their inferiors and were, in return, addressed as *you*. Gonzalo, for example, tells the boatswain 'Good, yet remember whom thou hast aboard' (I. 1.19), to which the boatswain replies 'None that I more love than myself. You are a counsellor; if you can command these elements to silence, and work the peace of the presence, we will not hand a rope more' (I.1.20–4). The use of *thou* could, depending on the situation, indicate that the speaker was talking to an intimate and so, as we would expect, it is the form used by Prospero when speaking to Miranda 'I have done nothing but in care of thee, / Of thee, my dear one; thee, my daughter' (I.2.16–17). When used inappropriately, however, *thou* could imply an insult.

- One further pronominal difference which may be noted is the use of *it* to refer to a person. In I.2.311, Miranda describes Caliban thus: ''Tis a villain, sir', and in III.2.101 Stephano uses *it* to refer to Miranda: 'Is it so brave a lass?'.

PREPOSITIONS

In Shakespeare's day, prepositional usage was less standardised than it is now, and so many of the writer's prepositions differ from those we would employ today. Among these are:

Preposition in *The Tempest*	Preferred modern usage	Reference
And suck'd my verdure out **on**'t	And sucked my health out of it	I.2.87
on a trice	in a trice, at the speed of light	V.1.238
Tunis was never grac'd before with such a paragon **to** their Queen	Tunis was never before graced with such a paragon for a queen	II.1.71–2
she was **of** Carthage, not **of** Tunis	she was from Carthage, not Tunis	II.1.79
with a twink	in the twinkling of an eye	IV.1.43

MULTIPLE NEGATION

In contemporary English, we normally use only one negative in a sentence, but in Shakespeare's day two or even more negatives could be used for emphasis. His sonnet 'Let me not to the marriage of true minds', for example, concludes with the following couplet: 'If this be error and upon me proved, / I **never** writ, **nor no** man ever loved.'

In *The Tempest* we find many examples of double negatives, among them the following: 'This is **no** mortal business **nor no** sound / That the earth owes' (I.2.409–10), and '**Nor** go **neither**; but you'll lie, like dogs, and yet say **nothing neither**' (III.2.18–19).

SPELLING AND PUNCTUATION

Contemporary spelling and punctuation are markedly different from Shakespeare's usage. This aspect of his work need not, however, detain us because almost all modern editions make use of contemporary conventions. To illustrate, the differences, however, we shall quote three verses of the story of Babel from the *King James **Bible*** of 1611:

1611 Version of Genesis 11:4–7

4 And they said; Goe to, let vs build vs a city and a tower, whose top may reach vnto heauen, and let vs make vs a name, lest we be scattered abroad vpon the face of the whole earth. 5 And the LORD came downe to see the city and the tower, which the children of men builded. 6 And the LORD said; Behold, the people is one, and they have all one language: and this they begin to doe: and now nothing will be restrained from them, which they haue imagined to doe.

Contemporary Version

4 And they said: 'So, let us build a city and a tower whose top will reach to the sky, and let us immortalise our name in case we are scattered far and wide. 5 And the Lord came down to see the city and the tower that the children of men had built. 6 And the Lord said: 'Look, the people are united and they all speak one language and they have begun to do such wonders. From now on they will be able to do anything that they put their mind to.'

The style of *The Tempest* is reminiscent of several of Shakespeare's final plays. It includes poetry of great beauty and elegiac notes that might, in an earlier period, have produced a tragedy. It is not 'realistic' in the sense of giving the audience a clear idea of life in seventeenth-century England but it raises issues that were, and are, relevant. We may criticise the unnaturalness of some of the episodes; we may worry about inconsistencies in characters and attitudes; but, like other pieces of great literature, it can evoke what Wordsworth called 'The still, sad music of humanity' (*Tintern Abbey*).

IMAGERY AND SYMBOLISM

Creative writers enjoy considerable freedom in their use of language in that they can mould and manipulate it to suit their literary purposes. Poetic language derives from ordinary, everyday speech but differs from it in that its purpose is not merely to communicate facts but also to delight and impress its audience by exploiting the resources of the language to the full. Poetic language differs from literary prose in that it is often rhythmically regular. We can compare, for example, the regular stress pattern of Ariel's comment to Prospero: 'Not a hair perish'd; / On their sustaining garments not a blemish, / But fresher than before: and, as thou bad'st me. / In troops I have dispers'd them 'bout the isle' (I.2.217–20), with the more speech-like prose statement of Stephano: 'Where the devil should learn our language? I will give him some relief, if it be but for that. If I can recover him, and keep him tame, and get to Naples with him, he's a present for any emperor that ever trod on neat's-leather' (II.2.67–72).

It is probably true to say that *The Tempest* is more concerned with the exploration of ideas, especially those associated with sin, repentance, purgation, than with the development of interlocking images. But the use of images is basic to all vivid language and can occur in poetry and prose alike.

IMAGERY

In *The Tempest* we find recurrent images of the sea. For example: 'The sky, it seems, would pour down stinking pitch, / But that the sea, mounting to th' welkin's cheek, / Dashes the fire out' (I.2.3–5), and 'Nothing of him that doth fade, / But doth suffer a sea-change / Into something rich and strange' (I.2.402–4).

We also find a wide range of images connected with the body (sometimes associated with the sea), especially the internal workings of the body or the pains inflicted on it. For example: 'Thou dost, and think'st it much to tread the ooze / Of the salt deep, / To run upon the sharp wind of the north, / To do me business in the veins o' th' earth / When it is bak'd with frost' (I.2.252–6), and 'You cram these words into mine ears against / The stomach of my sense' (II.1.102–3), or, in Prospero's threats to Caliban: 'For this, be sure, tonight thou shalt have cramps, / Side stitches that shall pen thy breath up' (I.2.327–8).

Simile and metaphor

Both similes and **metaphors** are often found in literary language because they allow the writer to extend the range of references. If Shakespeare, for example, says that love is like war or life is like the sea, he can then use images of war and of the sea when describing love and life. Similes and metaphors involve comparisons. With similes the comparison is overt. We say that one thing is like another or has some of the qualities of something else. Thus Gonzalo uses a simile when he compares the guilt of the three men of sin to poison: 'All three of them are desperate: their great guilt, / Like poison given to work a great time after, / Now 'gins to bite the spirits' (III.3.104–6). Prospero uses another when he tells Ariel he will soon be free: 'Thou shalt be as free / As mountain winds' (I.2.501–2).

With metaphor, the comparison is implied rather than stated. When, in *Macbeth*, Shakespeare wrote that the brevity of life resembled the short existence of a candle which can be put out at any moment, he was using metaphor. Metaphors are used in all varieties of language and numerous examples can be found in *The Tempest*. Gonzalo uses metaphor when he personifies Nature in a description of his ideal world:

> All things in common Nature should produce
> Without sweat or endeavour: treason, felony,
> Sword, pike, knife? gun? or need of any engine?
> Would I not have; but Nature should bring forth,
> Of it own kind, all foison, all abundance,
> To feed my innocent people. (II.1.154–9)

There are three metaphors in Antonio's temptation speech when he speaks of steel as if it could obey, when he compares death to an eternal wink and when Gonzalo is described as a morsel:

> Here lies your brother,
> No better than the earth he lies upon,
> If he were that which now he's like, that's dead;
> Whom I, with this obedient steel, three inches of it?
> Can lay to bed for ever; whiles you, doing thus,
> To the perpetual wink for aye might put
> This ancient morsel? (II.1.275–82)

WORD PLAY

Playing on different meanings of the same word or on words which sound alike has been popular in English literature since the time of Chaucer. Shakespeare and his contemporaries employed word play as a literary technique and also for the amusement and intellectual pleasure it seems to have given their audience. Examples of word play can be found throughout *The Tempest*, especially in the scenes which provide comic relief. We find it in I.2.83–5, for example, when Prospero utilises two meanings of 'key', an object which can open a door and the pitch of a melody: 'having both the key / Of officer and office, set all hearts i' th' state / To what tune pleas'd his ear', and later, in III.1.83–6, Miranda plays on the two meanings of 'maid', a domestic servant and a virgin: 'I am your wife if you will marry me; / If not, I'll die your maid: to be your fellow / You may deny me; but I'll be your servant, / Whether you will or no'.

DRAMATIC IRONY

This term is applied to an episode in a play where the audience can see more significance in the words of a character than the other characters can. In I.2.463–7, for example, Miranda and Ferdinand take Prospero's criticisms at face value:

> Speak not you for him: he's a traitor.
> Come; I'll manacle thy neck and feet together:
> Sea-water shalt thou drink; thy food shall be
> The fresh-brook mussels, wither'd roots, and husks
> Wherein the acorn cradled.

However the audience realises that Prospero has arranged the meeting between Ferdinand and his daughter in the hope that they would fall in love and thus heal the breach between Naples and Milan. The punishment is so that Ferdinand will not feel that Miranda was won too easily.

SYMBOLISM

When Shakespeare encourages us to see a character or an occurrence as representing another level of meaning, then he is making use of

symbolism. It is a technique that allows him to express abstract ideas through physical **imagery**. The very title of this play is symbolic in that it suggests turbulent relationships as well as a storm at sea; the animal imagery associated with Caliban may well be symbolic of Prospero's attitude to him; and the airs, both musical and physical, that are a feature of Ariel may suggest the spirit freed from physical limitations.

The language of *The Tempest* is less image-laden than many of Shakespeare's other dramas. Instead of a preponderance of images of decay, for example, that we find in *King Lear*, we find an interest in themes and ideas often underlined by the repetition of such key words as 'beauty', 'brave', 'nature', 'noble' and 'virtue'.

It has often been suggested that the **action** in *The Tempest* is not true to life, that the shipwreck, love affair and final reconciliation could not possibly have occurred in four hours. It is worth remembering, however, that a marriage ends a Shakespearean comedy or **tragicomedy** just as surely as deaths end a tragedy. In addition, one does not look to literature for chronological precision or logical exactness. The truth which has value in a work of art is a truth which imposes a coherence on the many narrative strands that are woven together by the artist.

PART FOUR

TEXTUAL ANALYSIS

Three passages have been selected from *The Tempest* to illustrate different aspects of the text, for example, dialogue and monologue, verse and prose, and to examine some themes and techniques (see Critical Approaches). The information is in note form so that you can be guided by suggestions, rather than influenced by essays that espouse a particular point of view.

TEXT 1 (I.1.1–67)

SCENE I. – [*On a ship at sea*]: *a tempestuous noise of thunder and lightning heard.*

Enter a Ship-Master and a Boatswain.

MASTER: Boatswain!

BOATSWAIN: Here, master: what cheer?

MASTER: Good: speak to th' mariners: fall to 't, yarely, or we run ourselves aground: bestir, bestir.

Exit.

Enter Mariners.

BOATSWAIN: Heigh, my hearts! cheerly, cheerly, my hearts! yare, yare! Take in the topsail. Tend to th' master's whistle. Blow till thou burst thy wind, if room enough!

Enter ALONSO, SEBASTIAN, ANTONIO, FERDINAND, GONZALO, *and others.*

ALONSO: Good boatswain, have care. Where's the master? Play the men.

BOATSWAIN: I pray now, keep below.

ANTONIO: Where is the master, boatswain?

BOATSWAIN: Do you not hear him? You mar our labour: keep your cabins: you do assist the storm.

GONZALO: Nay, good, be patient.

BOATSWAIN: When the sea is. Hence! What care these roarers for the name of the King? To cabin: silence! trouble us not.

GONZALO:Good, yet remember whom thou hast aboard.

BOATSWAIN: None that I more love than myself. You are a counsellor; if you can command these elements to silence, and work the peace of the presence, we will not hand a rope more; use your authority: if you cannot, give thanks you have lived so long, and make yourself ready in your cabin for the mischance of the hour, if it so hap. Cheerly, good hearts ! Out of our way, I say.

Exit.

GONZALO: I have great comfort from this fellow: methinks he hath no drowning mark upon him; his complexion is perfect gallows. Stand fast, good Fate, to his hanging: make the rope of his destiny our cable, for our own doth little advantage. If he be not born to be hanged, our case is miserable.

Exeunt.

Re-enter Boatswain.

BOATSWAIN: Down with the topmast! yare! lower, lower! Bring her to try with main-course. *A cry within.* A plague upon this howling! they are louder than the weather or our office.

[*Re-*]*enter* SEBASTIAN, ANTONIO, *and* GONZALO.

Yet again! what do you here? Shall we give o'er, and drown? Have you a mind to sink?

SEBASTIAN: A pox o' your throat, you bawling, blasphemous, incharitable dog!

BOATSWAIN: Work you, then.

ANTONIO: Hang, cur! hang, you whoreson, insolent noisemaker. We are less afraid to be drowned than thou art.

GONZALO: I'll warrant him for drowning, though the ship were no stronger than a nutshell, and as leaky as an unstanched wench.

BOATSWAIN: Lay her a-hold, a-hold! set her two courses; off to sea again; lay her off.

Enter Mariners wet.

MARINERS: All lost, to prayers, to prayers! all lost!

BOATSWAIN: What, must our mouths be cold?

GONZALO: The King and Prince at prayers, let's assist them,
For our case is as theirs.

SEBASTIAN: I'm out of patience.

ANTONIO: We are merely cheated of our lives by drunkards:
This wide-chapp'd rascal, – would thou mightst lie drowning
The washing of ten tides!

GONZALO: He'll be hang'd yet,
Though every drop of water swear against it,
And gape at wid'st to glut him.

A confined noise within: "Mercy on us!" –
"We split, we split!" – "Farewell, my wife and children!" –
"Farewell, brother!" – "We split, we split, we split!"

ANTONIO: Let's all sink wi' th' King.

SEBASTIAN: Let's take leave of him.

Exeunt [ANTONIO *and* SEBASTIAN].

GONZALO: Now would I give a thousand furlongs of sea for an acre of barren ground, long heath, broom, furze, anything. The wills above be done ! but I would fain die a dry death.

Exeunt.

This passage comes from the beginning of the play and is meant to capture and hold the attention of the audience, to introduce some of the characters and themes, and to suggest the nature of the drama about to unfold.

CHARACTERS: In spite of the confusion caused by danger, this passage allows us to make a number of deductions about the characters introduced:

- Some of them are designated by their trade, e.g. 'Boatswain' and 'Master', whereas others have first names such as Alonso and Gonzalo. An obvious inference from this is that the audience will get to know the latter group. These are characters whose story is about to unfold.
- The courtly characters are, perhaps, so used to being obeyed that they attempt to interfere in the Master's attempts to ride the storm. Even

within this broad generalisation, however, we can detect three distinct attitudes. Alonso is worried but courteous ('Good boatswain, have care' – line 9); Antonio and Sebastian are inconsiderate and rude ('A pox o'your throat' – line 40 – and 'whoreson, insolent noisemaker' – line 43) and they put their own safety before that of the king (line 63); and Gonzalo attempts to be a peacemaker (line 15), is talkative (line 28ff), good humoured (line 46ff), attentive to Alonso's needs (line 53) and willing to accept his fate with courage (lines 66–7).

Recurrent themes: Since these are the first words an audience hears, we would expect certain interests to be established. These include:
- The significance of the storm
- The potential feud between Alonso and his brother
- The willingness of Alonso to repent. He is, after all, 'at prayers' (line 53)
- The suggested closeness between Alonso and the prince in that they are together
- Gonzalo's loyalty to the king

The handling of time: Even in this short scene, there are indications of the quick passage of time:
- There are six entrances and five exits, suggesting a great deal of activity over a period of time
- The Boatswain gives instructions that must take time to carry out
- There is time for the king to attempt to find out what is happening and then go below to pray
- Antonio and Sebastian can decide not to drown with the king but to save themselves

The language and style: The language is relatively easy to understand in context, although some of the vocabulary and many of the structures are no longer current.
- A modern audience would have to guess the meaning of such words as 'yarely', 'bestir', 'cheerly', 'roarers', but might notice that such words are more likely to occur in the speech of the mariners.
- It might also notice the use of 'do' where it seems unnecessary, as in 'you do assist the storm' (line 14), and its non-use in forming questions: 'What care these roarers?' (line 16).

TEXT 1 continued

- Speed is indicated in the use of orders rather than statements and in the reduction of structures, e.g. 'if room enough' (if there is room enough) and 'have care' (have a care) (lines 7–9).
- An attentive observer might notice that Gonzalo uses 'thou' to the Boatswain but receives 'you' back (lines 19–26), thus stressing the difference in rank.
- Alonso's style of address is courteous; the mariners are unwilling to tolerate interference even from people of much higher rank.

THE IMAGERY AND SYMBOLISM: The most significant images here are of struggle and suffering:
- The strength and noise of the storm (e.g. line 8, line 36 and line 47)
- Death by drowning (line 29)
- Death by hanging (line 30)
- Barrenness (line 65)

TEXT 2 (I.2.285–345)

PROSPERO: Dull thing, I say so; he, that Caliban,
Whom now I keep in service. Thou best know'st
What torment I did find thee in; thy groans
Did make wolves howl, and penetrate the breasts
Of ever-angry bears: it was a torment
To lay upon the damn'd, which Sycorax
Could not again undo: it was mine Art,
When I arriv'd and heard thee, that made gape
The pine, and let thee out.

ARIEL: I thank thee, master.

PROSPERO: If thou more murmur'st, I will rend an oak,
And peg thee in his knotty entrails, till
Thou hast howl'd away twelve winters.

ARIEL: Pardon, master:
I will be correspondent to command,
And do my spriting gently.

PROSPERO: Do so; and after two days
I will discharge thee.

ARIEL: That's my noble master!
What shall I do? say what; what shall I do?

PROSPERO: Go make thyself like a nymph o' th' sea:
Be subject to
No sight but thine and mine; invisible
To every eyeball else. Go take this shape,
And hither come in't: go: hence
With diligence.

Exit [ARIEL]

Awake, dear heart, awake! thou hast slept well;
Awake!

MIRANDA: The strangeness of your story put
Heaviness in me.

PROSPERO: Shake it off. Come on;
We'll visit Caliban my slave, who never
Yields us kind answer.

MIRANDA: 'Tis a villain, sir,
I do not love, to look on.

PROSPERO: But, as 'tis,
We cannot miss him: he does make our fire,
Fetch in our wood, and serves in offices
That profit us. What, ho! slave! Caliban!
Thou earth, thou! speak.

CALIBAN: *within.* There's wood enough within.

PROSPERO: Come forth, I say! there's other business for thee;
Come, thou tortoise! when?
[*Re-*]*enter* ARIEL *like a water-nymph.*
Fine apparition! My quaint Ariel
Hark in thine ear.

ARIEL: My lord, it shall be done.

Exit.

PROSPERO: Thou poisonous slave, got by the devil himself
Upon thy wicked dam, come forth!
Enter CALIBAN.

CALIBAN: As wicked dew as e'er my mother brush'd
With raven's feather from unwholesome fen
Drop on you both! a south-west blow on ye
And blister you all o'er!

PROSPERO: For this, be sure, to-night thou shalt have cramps,
Side-stitches that shall pen thy breath up; urchins
Shall, for that vast of night that they may work,
All exercise on thee; thou shalt be pinch'd
As thick as honeycomb, each pinch more stinging
Than bees that made 'em.

CALIBAN: I must eat my dinner.
This island's mine, by Sycorax my mother,
Which thou tak'st from me. When thou cam'st first,
Thou strok'st me, and made much of me; wouldst give me
Water with berries in 't; and teach me how
To name the bigger light, and how the less,
That burn by day and night: and then I lov'd thee,
And show'd thee all the qualities o' th' isle,
The fresh springs, brine-pits, barren place and fertile:
Curs'd be I that did so! All the charms
Of Sycorax, toads, beetles, bats, light on you!
For I am all the subjects that you have,
Which first was mine own King: and here you sty me
In this hard rock, whiles you do keep from me
The rest o' th' island.

This passage comes from the second scene of the first act and is significant in introducing the audience to the island dwellers. Prospero's power is stressed and perhaps the audience is encouraged to think of Prospero as a godlike figure, whose power one admires but whose actions are not always understood. We are also invited to compare and contrast Prospero's attitude to Ariel and to Caliban.

CHARACTERS: The characters reveal themselves in what they say and how they say it, what they do and how they do it, and in their behaviour towards others.

- Prospero's first words 'Dull thing' reduce Caliban from a person to an inanimate object.

- He controls Ariel more by a technique known as 'carrot and stick' (line 299 offers freedom and line 295 the pain of being imprisoned)
- Prospero's attitude to Miranda is much kinder ('dear heart', line 307) but she is kept totally in the dark about Ariel, who must remain invisible to everyone but Prospero (line 302).
- Prospero needs Caliban's work (lines 313-14) but treats him as a 'slave' (line 315), as lazy and slow (line 317) and insults his mother, whom he suggests mated with the devil (line 321ff).
- Miranda clearly states her dislike of Caliban (lines 311-12) but her use of 'It' in line 311, ''Tis a villain', should not be misunderstood. In Shakespeare's day, 'it' was frequently used where we would use 'he' (see Language and Style).
- Caliban may be enslaved but his speech is anything but servile. He is prepared to suffer excruciating cramps (line 326) rather than accept the insult to his mother. His belief in his right to the island is one of the first things we hear him say (line 333). Whereas Ariel is prepared to do everything that Prospero wants as a means of gaining eventual freedom, Caliban insists that he should not have to earn his freedom because the island, and all that it produces, is his.

Recurrent themes: These four characters are among the most important in the play and Shakespeare associates them with the major themes:
- Prospero: magic ('mine Art' - line 291) and power, often cruel (lines 295 and 327)
- Miranda: innocence (line 307 shows that Miranda has no idea that her father used his powers to make her sleep)
- Ariel: beauty (line 301), speed (line 319), enjoyment of work (line 320)
- Caliban: courage and strength of character (lines 324-6), love of the island (lines 332ff), attitude towards coloniser (lines 334ff).

The handling of time: Although this part of Scene 2 can be acted in five minutes, we are given an impression of time passing by references to:
- The distant past when Sycorax was alive and Ariel trapped in a tree (line 286) and to the future when Ariel will be free (line 298)
- The more recent past when Prospero arrived and treated Caliban well (line 334)

- The regularity with which Caliban performs his menial tasks (line 313)
- The fact that Miranda has been asleep (line 307)
- The fact that Ariel can transform himself into a nymph (line 300)

THE LANGUAGE AND STYLE: This varies subtly to imply different attitudes, characters and topics:

- Ariel and Caliban both use 'thou' to Prospero, Ariel's use suggesting intimacy, Caliban's an unwillingness to accept his enslavement. Miranda uses 'you' to her father, stressing her respect.
- Prospero is used to being obeyed and uses more commands than any other character (lines 301ff, lines 317ff). He also uses 'I' more than the others, again suggesting his power and self absorption, especially since the 'I' frequently occurs with verbs of doing, punishing and rewarding.
- Miranda says very little here but shows respect for her father. She is much less critical of Caliban, saying only that he is a villain and that she does not like to see him.
- Ariel uses address terms such as 'master' (line 296) and 'lord' (line 320), suggesting that he is willing to appear servile if it wins his freedom.
- Caliban does not use one courteous term of address; he is prepared to suffer for the sake of cursing both Prospero and Miranda (lines 323ff). Caliban uses verse throughout, suggesting that, in spite of being enslaved, his spirit is free and he is keenly aware of natural beauty (lines 336ff).

THE IMAGERY AND SYMBOLISM: The imagery is associated with:

- Pain and suffering (threatened for Ariel and Caliban by Prospero and in Caliban's curse)
- Beauty (line 301)
- Animal imagery, e.g. wolves, beasts, bears, tortoise, raven, bees, toads, beetles, bats. These are, with the exception of the first three, associated with Caliban. Notice that only the first three are dangerous mammals whereas the others might be seen as lower-order animals, suggesting Prospero's attitude to Caliban's position in the natural hierarchy.

TEXT 3 (II.1.15–74)

MIRANDA: Alas now, pray you,
Work not so hard: I would the lightning had
Burnt up those logs that you are enjoin'd to pile!
Pray, set it down, and rest you: when this burns,
'Twill weep for having wearied you. My father
Is hard at study; pray, now, rest yourself:
He's safe for these three hours.

FERDINAND: O most dear mistress,
The sun will set before I shall discharge
What I must strive to do.

MIRANDA: If you'll sit down,
I'll bear your logs the while: pray give me that;
I'll carry it to the pile.

FERDINAND: No, precious creature;
I had rather crack my sinews, break my back,
Than you should such dishonour undergo,
While I sit lazy by.

MIRANDA: It would become me
As well as it does you: and I should do it
With much more ease; for my good will is to it,
And yours it is against.

PROSPERO: Poor worm thou art infected!
This visitation shows it.

MIRANDA: You look wearily.

FERDINAND: No, noble mistress: 'tis fresh morning with me
When you are by at night. I do beseech you, -
Chiefly that I might set it in my prayers, -
What is your name?

MIRANDA: Miranda. - O my father,
I have broke your hest to say so!

FERDINAND: Admir'd Miranda!
Indeed the top of admiration! worth
What's dearest to the world! Full many a lady
I have ey'd with best regard, and many a time
Th' harmony of their tongues hath into bondage
Brought my too diligent ear: for several virtues
Have I lik'd several women; never any
With so full soul, but some defect in her
Did quarrel with the noblest grace she ow'd,
And put it to the foil: but you, O you,
So perfect and so peerless, are created
Of every creature's best!

MIRANDA: I do not know
One of my sex; no woman's face remember,
Save, from my glass, mine own; nor have I seen
More that I may call men than you, good friend,
And my dear father: how features are abroad,
I am skilless of; but, by my modesty,
The jewel in my dower, I would not wish
Any companion in the world but you;
Nor can imagination form a shape,
Besides yourself, to like of. But I prattle
Something too wildly, and my father's precepts
I therein do forget.

FERDINAND: I am, in my condition,
A prince, Miranda; I do think, a King;
I would not so! - and would no more endure
This wooden slavery than to suffer
The flesh-fly blow my mouth. Hear my soul speak:
The very instant that I saw you, did
My heart fly to your service; there resides,
To make me slave to it; and for your sake
Am I this patient log-man.

MIRANDA: Do you love me?

ferdinand: O heaven, O earth, bear witness to this sound,
And crown what I profess with kind event,
If I speak true! if hollowly, invert
What best is boded me to mischief! I,
Beyond all limit of what else i' th' world,
Do love, prize, honour you.

miranda: I am a fool
To weep at what I am glad of

The final passage is a dialogue between the two young lovers. Ferdinand has been forced to carry logs so that Prospero can test the depth of his regard for Miranda and prevent him thinking that Miranda is too easily won. Prospero watches the two and is moved by their gentle consideration of each other.

Characters: Only the audience is aware that there are three characters in this scene and it is possible to regard Prospero either as a 'peeping tom' or as a father who wants only the best for his innocent daughter. (You might like to compare the scene in Milton's *Paradise Lost* where Satan enters the Garden of Eden and watches Adam and Eve before the fall. He is so struck by their beauty and innocence that, in Milton's words, he sat 'stupidly good'.)

- Miranda is generous and considerate, willing to share Ferdinand's punishment. He is equally determined that he will not allow her to suffer on his behalf.
- There is no artifice in Miranda. She responds to Ferdinand's compliments by saying that she loves him and would like to bc his wife (lines 55ff). Indeed, she is the one who moves their relationship along by asking 'Do you love me?' (line 67).
- Ferdinand stresses his love by saying that, although he is a prince, he is glad to labour for her sake (lines 60-65).

Recurrent themes: Love, in its many forms, is thematic in *The Tempest*. This scene reveals:

- Falling in love and the development of love between Miranda and Ferdinand, shown in their kindness to each other and their willingness to suffer for each other
- Love of a father for a daughter

- The inter-relationship between love and power: Prospero plans the love in order to win back his dukedom; Ferdinand is willing to forego his princedom if it means he can have Miranda.

THE HANDLING OF TIME: Time is of little significance to the lovers but it is indicated by:
- Ferdinand's references to other women he has known (lines 39ff)
- Miranda's stressing her ignorance of men
- Prospero's reference to the fact that Miranda has been 'infected' (line 31)

THE LANGUAGE AND STYLE: The interchanges between Miranda and Ferdinand are among the most poetic in the play. They use 'you' to each other, stressing their mutual respect but also emphasising the fact that they have not known each other long. Their dialogue is a series of questions and answers where they provide each other and the audience with information about the past and with a clear indication of the beauty of their characters.

THE IMAGERY AND SYMBOLISM: Apart from Prospero's reference to Miranda as a 'poor worm' (line 31) there is no animal imagery here. Instead, we find references to:
- Pain (line 16)
- Natural phenomena: lightning (line 16), fresh morning (line 33), night (line 34)
- Music (line 41)
- Body parts: eyes, tongues, ears (lines 40ff)
- Jewels (lines 54ff)

The textual analyses above are not meant to be exhaustive. They show only how the themes and techniques described in Critical Approaches are useful tools in the response to, and description of, texts.

Part five

Background

William shakespeare's life

There are no personal records of Shakespeare's life. Official documents and occasional references to him by contemporary dramatists enable us to draw the main outline of his public life, but his private life remains hidden. Although not at all unusual for a writer of his time, this lack of first-hand evidence has tempted many to read his plays as personal records and to look in them for clues to his character and convictions. The results are unconvincing, partly because Renaissance art was not subjective or designed primarily to express its creator's personality, and partly because the drama of any period is very difficult to read biographically. Except when plays are written by committed dramatists to promote social or political causes (as by Shaw or Brecht), it is all but impossible to decide who amongst the variety of fictional characters in a drama represents the dramatist, or which of the various and often conflicting points of view expressed is authorial.

What we do know can be quickly summarised. Shakespeare was born into a well-to-do family in the market town of Stratford-upon-Avon in Warwickshire, where he was baptised, in Holy Trinity Church, on 26 April 1564. His father, John Shakespeare, was a prosperous glover and leather merchant who became a person of some importance in the town: in 1565 he was elected an alderman, and in 1568 he became high bailiff (or mayor) of Stratford. In 1557 he had married Mary Arden. Their third child (of eight) and eldest son, William, learned to read and write at the primary (or 'petty') school in Stratford and then, it seems probable, attended the local grammar school, where he would have studied Latin, history, logic and rhetoric. In November 1582 William, then aged eighteen, married Anne Hathaway, who was twenty-six years old. They had a daughter, Susanna, in May 1583, and twins, Hamnet and Judith, in 1585.

Shakespeare next appears in the historical record in 1592 when he was mentioned as a London actor and playwright in a pamphlet by the dramatist Robert Greene. These 'lost years' 1585–92 have been the subject of much speculation, but how they were occupied remains as much a mystery as when Shakespeare left Stratford, and why. In his pamphlet,

Greene's Groatsworth of Wit, Greene expresses to his fellow dramatists his outrage that the 'upstart crow' Shakespeare has the impudence to believe he 'is as well able to bombast out a blank verse as the best of you'. To have aroused this hostility from a rival, Shakespeare must, by 1592, have been long enough in London to have made a name for himself as a playwright. We may conjecture that he had left Stratford in 1586 or 1587.

During the next twenty years, Shakespeare continued to live in London, regularly visiting his wife and family in Stratford. He continued to act, but his chief fame was as a dramatist. From 1594 he wrote exclusively for the Lord Chamberlain's Men, which rapidly became the leading dramatic company and from 1603 enjoyed the patronage of James I as the King's Men. His plays were extremely popular and he became a shareholder in his theatre company. He was able to buy lands around Stratford and a large house in the town, to which he retired about 1611. He died there on 23 April 1616 and was buried in Holy Trinity Church on 25 April.

SHAKESPEARE'S DRAMATIC CAREER

Between the late 1580s and 1613 Shakespeare wrote thirty-seven plays, and contributed to some by other dramatists. This was by no means an exceptional number for a professional playwright of the times. The exact date of the composition of individual plays is a matter of debate – for only a few plays is the date of their first performance known – but the broad outlines of Shakespeare's dramatic career have been established. He began in the late 1580s and early 1590s by rewriting earlier plays and working with plotlines inspired by the Classics. He concentrated on comedies (such as *The Comedy of Errors*, 1590–4, which derived from the Latin playwright Plautus) and plays dealing with English history (such as the three parts of *Henry VI*, 1589–92), though he also tried his hand at bloodthirsty revenge tragedy (*Titus Andronicus*, 1592–3, indebted to both Ovid and Seneca). During the 1590s Shakespeare developed his expertise in these kinds of play to write such comic masterpieces such as *A Midsummer Night's Dream* (1594–5) and *As You Like It* (1599–1600) and history plays such as *Henry IV* (1596–8) and *Henry V* (1598–9).

As the new century begins a new note is detectable. Plays such as *Troilus and Cressida* (1601–2) and *Measure for Measure* (1603–4), poised between comedy and tragedy, evoke complex responses. Because of their generic uncertainty and ambivalent tone such works are sometimes referred to as 'problem plays', but it is tragedy which comes to dominate the extraordinary sequence of masterpieces: *Hamlet* (1600–1), *Othello* (1602–4), *King Lear* (1605–6), *Macbeth* (1605–6) and *Antony and Cleopatra* (1606).

In the last years of his dramatic career, Shakespeare wrote a group of plays of a quite different kind. These 'romances', as they are often called, are in many ways the most remarkable of all his plays. The group comprises *Pericles* (1608), *Cymbeline* (1609–11), *The Winter's Tale* (1610–11) and *The Tempest* (1610–11). These plays (particularly *Cymbeline*) reprise many of the situations and themes of the earlier dramas but in fantastical and exotic dramatic designs which, set in distant lands, covering large tracts of time and involving music, mime, dance and tableaux, have something of the qualities of masques and pageants. The situations which in the tragedies had led to disaster are here resolved: the great theme is restoration and reconciliation. Where in the tragedies Ophelia, Desdemona and Cordelia died, the daughters of these plays – Marina, Imogen, Perdita, Miranda – survive and are reunited with their parents and lovers.

THE TEXTS OF SHAKESPEARE'S PLAYS

Nineteen of Shakespeare's plays were printed during his lifetime in what are called 'quartos' (books, each containing one play, and made up of sheets of paper each folded twice to make four leaves). Shakespeare, however, did not supervise their publication. This was not unusual. When a playwright had sold a play to a dramatic company he sold his rights in it: copyright belonged to whoever had possession of an actual copy of the text, and so consequently authors had no control over what happened to their work. Anyone who could get hold of the text of a play might publish it if they wished. Hence, what found its way into print might be the author's copy, but it might be an actor's copy or prompt copy, perhaps cut or altered for performance; sometimes, actors (or even members of the audience) might publish what they could remember of the text. Printers, working without the benefit of the author's oversight, introduced their own errors, through misreading the manuscript, for example, and by 'correcting' what seemed to them not to make sense.

THE GLOBE THEATRE,

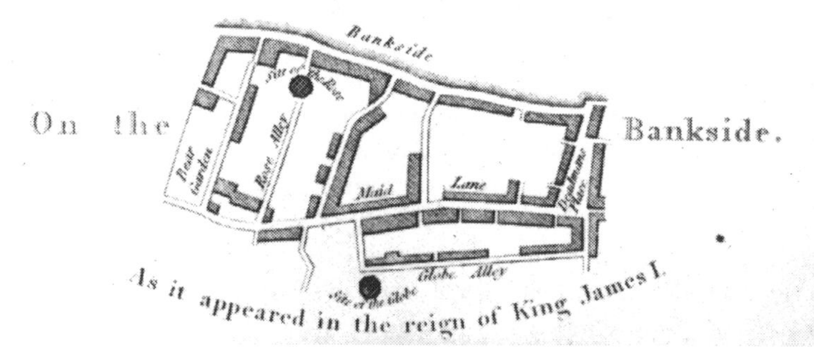

On the Bankside.
As it appeared in the reign of King James I.

GLOBE THEATRE

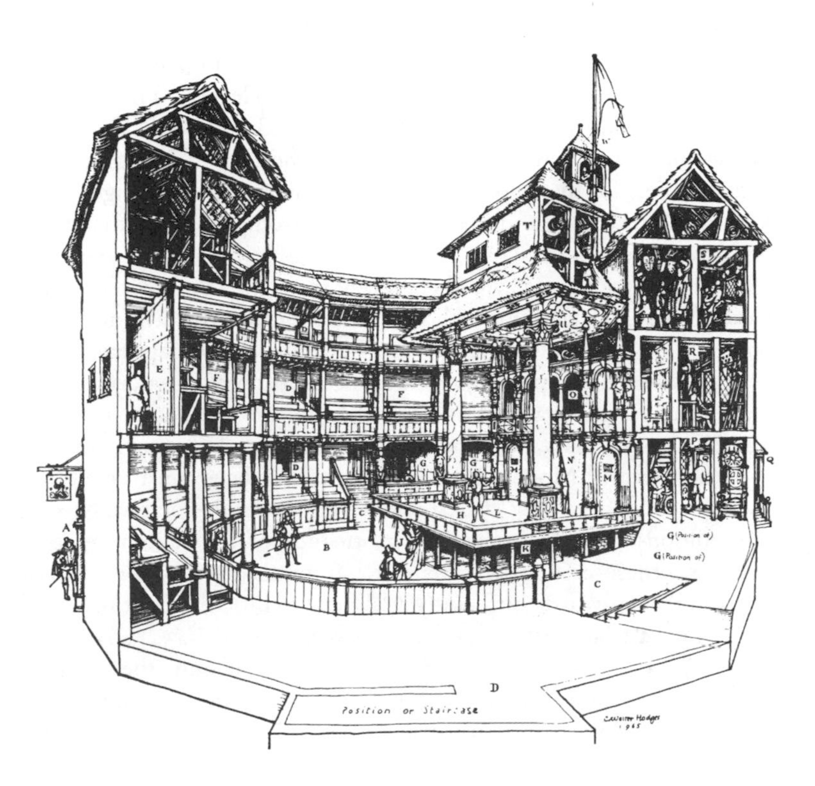

A CONJECTURAL RECONSTRUCTION OF THE INTERIOR OF THE GLOBE PLAYHOUSE

AA Main entrance
B The Yard
CC Entrances to lowest galleries
D Entrance to staircase and upper galleries
E Corridor serving the different sections of the middle gallery
F Middle gallery ('Twopenny Rooms')
G 'Gentlemen's Rooms or Lords Rooms'
H The stage
J The hanging being put up round the stage
K The 'Hell' under the stage
L The stage trap, leading down to the Hell
MM Stage doors
N Curtained 'place behind the stage'
O Gallery above the stage, used as required sometimes by musicians, sometimes by spectators, and often as part of the play
P Back-stage area (the tiring-house)
Q Tiring-house door
R Dressing-rooms
S Wardrobe and storage
T The hut housing the machine for lowering enthroned gods, etc., to the stage
U The 'Heavens'
W Hoisting the playhouse flag

In 1623 John Heminges and Henry Condell, two actors in Shakespeare's company, collected together texts of thirty-six of Shakespeare's plays (*Pericles* was omitted) and published them in a large folio (a book in which each sheet of paper is folded once in half, to give two leaves). This, the First Folio, was followed by later editions in 1632, 1663 and 1685. Despite its appearance of authority, however, the texts in the First Folio still present many difficulties, for there are printing errors and confused passages in the plays, and its texts often differ significantly from those of the earlier quartos, when these exist.

Shakespeare's texts have, then, been through a number of intermediaries. We do not have his authority for any one of his plays, and hence we cannot know exactly what it was that he wrote. Bibliographers, textual critics and editors have spent a great deal of effort on endeavouring to get behind the errors, uncertainties and contradictions in the available texts to recover the plays as Shakespeare originally wrote them. What we read is the result of these efforts. Modern texts are what editors have constructed from the available evidence: they correspond to no sixteenth- or seventeenth-century editions, and to no early performance of a Shakespeare play. Furthermore, these composite texts differ from each other, for different editors read the early texts differently and come to different conclusions. A Shakespeare text is an unstable and a contrived thing.

Often, of course, its judgements embody, if not the personal prejudices of the editor, then the cultural preferences of the time in which he or she was working. Growing awareness of this has led recent scholars to distrust the whole editorial enterprise and to repudiate the attempt to construct a 'perfect' text. Stanley Wells and Gary Taylor, the editors of the Oxford edition of *The Complete Works* (1988), point out that almost certainly the texts of Shakespeare's plays were altered in performance, and from one performance to another, so that there may never have been a single version. They note, too, that Shakespeare probably revised and rewrote some plays. They do not claim to print a definitive text of any play, but prefer what seems to them the 'more theatrical' version, and when there is a great difference between available versions, as with *King Lear*, they print two texts.

Shakespeare arrived in London at the very time that the Elizabethan period was poised to become the 'golden age' of English literature. Although Elizabeth reigned as queen from 1558 to 1603, the term 'Elizabethan' is used very loosely in a literary sense to refer to the period 1580 to 1625, when the great works of the age were produced. (Sometimes the later part of this period is distinguished as 'Jacobean', from the Latin form of James – James I of England and VI of Scotland reigned from 1603 to 1625.) The poet Edmund Spenser heralded this new age with his pastoral poem *The Shepheardes Calender* (1579) and in his essay *An Apologie for Poetrie* (written about 1580, although not published until 1595) his friend Sir Philip Sidney championed the imaginative power of the 'speaking picture of poesy', famously declaring that 'Nature never set forth the earth in so rich a tapestry as divers poets have done … Her world is brazen, the poet's only deliver a golden'.

Spenser and Sidney were part of that rejuvenating movement in European culture which since the nineteenth cnetury has been known by the term *Renaissance*. Meaning literally *rebirth*, it denotes a revival and redirection of artistic and intellectual endeavour which began in Italy in the fourteenth century in the poetry of **Petrarch**. It spread gradually northwards across Europe, and is first detectable in England in the early sixteenth century in the writings of the scholar and statesman Sir Thomas More and in the poetry of Sir Thomas Wyatt and Henry Howard, Earl of Surrey. Its keynote was a curiosity in thought which challenged old assumptions and traditions. To the innovative spirit of the Renaissance, the preceding ages appeared dully unoriginal and conformist.

That spirit was fuelled by the rediscovery of many Classical texts and the culture of Greece and Rome. This fostered a confidence in human reason and in human potential which, in every sphere, challenged old convictions. The discovery of America and its peoples (Columbus had sailed in 1492) demonstrated that the world was a larger and stranger place than had been thought. The cosmological speculation of Copernicus (later confirmed by Galileo) that the sun, not the earth was the centre of our planetary system challenged the centuries-old belief that the earth and human beings were at the centre of the cosmos. The pragmatic political philosophy of Machiavelli seemed to cut politics free from its traditional link with morality by permitting to statesmen any means which secured the desired end. And the religious movements we know collectively as the

Reformation broke with the Church of Rome and set the individual conscience, not ecclesiastical authority, at the centre of the religious life. Nothing, it seemed, was beyond questioning, nothing impossible.

Shakespeare's drama is innovative and challenging in exactly the way of the Renaissance. It questions the beliefs, assumptions and politics upon which Elizabethan society was founded. And although the plays always conclude in a restoration of order and stability, many critics are inclined to argue that their imaginative energy goes into subverting, rather than reinforcing, traditional values. They would point out that the famous speech on hierarchical order in *Troilus and Cressida* (I.3.86–124) or Katerina's speech on wifely submission to patriarchal authority in *The Taming of the Shrew* (V.2.146–60) appear to be rendered **ironic** by the action of the plays in which they occur. Convention, audience expectation and censorship all required the *status quo* to be endorsed by the plots' conclusions, but the dramas find ways to allow alternative sentiments to be expressed. Frequently, figures of authority are undercut by some comic or challenging figure: against the Duke in *Measure for Measure* is set Lucio; against Prospero in *The Tempest*, Caliban; against Henry IV, Falstaff. Despairing, critical, dissident, disillusioned, unbalanced, rebellious, mocking voices are repeatedly to be heard in the plays, rejecting, resenting, defying the established order. They belong always to marginal, socially unacceptable figures, 'licensed', as it were, by their situations to say what would be unacceptable from socially privileged or responsible citizens. The question is: are such characters given these views to discredit them, or were they the only ones through whom a voice could be given to radical and dissident ideas? Is Shakespeare a conservative or a revolutionary?

Renaissance culture was intensely nationalistic. With the break-up of the internationalism of the Middle Ages the evolving nation states which still mark the map of Europe began for the first time to acquire distinctive cultural identities. There was intense rivalry among them as they sought to achieve in their own vernacular languages a culture which could equal that of Greece and Rome. Spenser's great allegorical epic poem *The Faerie Queene*, which began to appear from 1590, celebrated Elizabeth and was intended to outdo the poetic achievements of France and Italy and to stand beside works of Virgil and Homer. Shakespeare is equally preoccupied with national identity. His history plays tell an epic story which examines how modern England came into being through the conflicts of the fifteenth-century Wars of the Roses which brought the Tudors to the throne. He is fascinated, too, by the related subject of politics and the exercise of power. With the collapse of medieval feudalism and the authority of local barons, the royal court in the Renaissance came to assume a new status as the centre of power and patronage. It was here that the destiny of a country was shaped. Courts, and how to succeed in them, consequently fascinated the Renaissance; and they fascinated Shakespeare and his audience.

That is why we are usually at court in his plays, and in the company of courtiers. But the dramatic gaze is not merely admiring; through a variety of devices, a critical perspective is brought to bear. The court may be paralleled by a very different world, revealing uncomfortable similarities (for example, Henry's court and the Boar's Head tavern, ruled over by Falstaff in *Henry IV*). Its hypocrisy may be bitterly denounced (for example, in the diatribes of the mad Lear) and its self-seeking ambition represented disturbingly in the figure of a Machiavellian villain (such as Edmund in *Lear*) or a malcontent (such as Iago in *Othello*). Shakespeare is fond of displacing the court to another context, the better to examine its assumptions and pretensions and to offer alternatives to the courtly life (for example, in the pastoral setting of the forest of Arden in *As You Like It* or Prospero's island in *The Tempest*). Courtiers are frequently figures of fun whose unmanly sophistication ('neat and trimly dressed, / Fresh as a bridegroom ... perfumed like a milliner', says Hotspur of such a man in *Henry IV*, I.3.33–6) is contrasted with plain-speaking integrity: Oswald is set against Kent in *King Lear*.

(When thinking of these matters, we should remember that stage plays were subject to censorship, and any criticism had therefore to be muted or oblique: direct criticism of the monarch or contemporary English court would not be tolerated. This has something to do with why Shakespeare's plays are always set either in the past, or abroad.)

The nationalism of the English Renaissance was reinforced by Protestantism. Henry VIII had broken with Rome in the 1530s and in Shakespeare's time there was an independent Protestant state church. Because the Pope in Rome had excommunicated Queen Elizabeth as a heretic and relieved the English of their allegiance to the Crown, there was deep suspicion of Roman Catholics as potential traitors. This was enforced by the attempted invasion of the Spanish Armada in 1588. This was a religiously inspired crusade to overthrow Elizabeth and restore England to

Roman Catholic allegiance. Roman Catholicism was hence often identified with hostility to England. Its association with disloyalty and treachery was enforced by the Gunpowder Plot of 1605, a Roman Catholic attempt to destroy the government of England.

Shakespeare's plays are remarkably free from direct religious sentiment, but their emphases are post-Reformation. Young women, for example, are destined for marriage, not for convents (precisely what Isabella appears to escape at the end of *Measure for Measure*; friars are ambiguous characters, even if with benign intentions, as in *Much Ado About Nothing* or *Romeo and Juliet*. The central figures of the plays are frequently individuals beset by temptation, by the lure of evil – Angelo in *Measure for Measure*, Othello, Lear, Macbeth – and not only in tragedies: Falstaff is described as 'that old white-bearded Satan' (*1 Henry IV*, II.4.454). We follow their inner struggles. Shakespeare's heroes have the preoccupation with self and the introspective tendencies often associated with Protestantism: his tragic heroes are haunted by their consciences, seeking their true selves, agonising over what course of action to take as they follow what can often be understood as a kind of spiritual progress towards heaven or hell.

SHAKESPEARE'S THEATRE

The theatre for which the plays were written was one of the most remarkable innovations of the Renaissance. There had been no theatres or acting companies during the medieval period. Performed on carts and in open spaces at Christian festivals, plays had been almost exclusively religious. Such professional actors as there were wandered the country putting on a variety of entertainments in the yards of inns, on makeshift stages in market squares, or anywhere else suitable. They did not perform full-length plays, but mimes, juggling and comedy acts. Such actors were regarded by officialdom and polite society as little better than vagabonds and layabouts.

Just before Shakespeare went to London all this began to change. A number of young men who had been to the universities of Oxford and Cambridge came to London in the 1580s and began to write plays which made use of what they had learned about the Classical drama of ancient Greece and Rome. Plays such as John Lyly's *Alexander and Campaspe* (1584), Christopher Marlowe's *Tamburlaine the Great* (about 1587) and

Thomas Kyd's *The Spanish Tragedy* (1588–9) were unlike anything that had been written in English before. They were full-length plays on secular subjects, taking their plots from history and legend, adopting many of the devices of Classical drama, and offering a range of characterisation and situation hitherto unattempted in English drama. With the exception of Lyly's prose dramas, they were in **blank verse** (unrhymed iambic pentameters) which the Earl of Surrey had introduced into English earlier in the sixteenth century. This was a freer and more expressive medium than the rhymed verse of medieval drama. It was the drama of these 'university wits' which Shakespeare challenged when he came to London. Greene was one of them, and we have heard how little he liked this Shakespeare setting himself up as a dramatist.

The most significant change of all, however, was that these dramatists wrote for the professional theatre. In 1576 James Burbage built the first permanent theatre in England, in Shoreditch, just beyond London's northern boundary. It was called simply 'The Theatre'. Others soon followed. Thus, when Shakespeare came to London, there was a flourishing drama, theatres and companies of actors waiting for him, such as there had never been before in England. His company performed at James Burbage's Theatre until 1596, and used the Swan and Curtain until they moved into their own new theatre, the Globe, in 1599. (The Globe was burned down in 1613 when a cannon was fired during a performance of Shakespeare's *Henry VIII*.) We know that *Romeo and Juliet* was played at the Curtain, and, as a popular play, it would have been presented at the Globe as well.

With the completion in 1996 of Sam Wanamaker's project to construct in London a replica of The Globe, and with productions now running there, a version of Shakespeare's theatre can be experienced at first hand. It is very different to the usual modern experience of drama. The form of the Elizabethan theatre derived from the inn yards and animal baiting rings in which actors had been accustomed to perform in the past. They were circular wooden buildings with a paved courtyard in the middle open to the sky. A rectangular stage jutted out into the middle of this yard. Some of the audience stood in the yard (or 'pit') to watch the play. They were thus on three sides of the stage, close up to it and on a level with it. These 'groundlings' paid only a penny to get in, but for wealthier spectators there were seats in three covered tiers or galleries between the inner and outer walls of the building, extending round most of the auditorium and overlooking the pit and the stage. Such a theatre could hold about 3,000 spectators. The yards were about 80ft in diameter and the rectangular stage approximately 40ft by 30ft and 5ft 6in high. Shakespeare aptly called such a theatre a 'wooden O' in the Prologue to *Henry V* (line 13).

The stage itself was partially covered by a roof or canopy which projected from the wall at the rear of the stage and was supported by two posts at the front. This protected the stage and performers from inclement weather, and to it were secured winches and other machinery for stage effects. On either side at the back of the stage was a door. These led into the dressing room (or 'tiring house') and it was by means of these doors that actors entered and left the stage. Between these doors was a small recess or alcove which was curtained off. Such a 'discovery place' served, for example, for Juliet's bedroom when in Act IV Scene 4 of *Romeo and Juliet* the Nurse went to the back of the stage and drew the curtain to find, or 'discover' in Elizabethan English, Juliet apparently dead on her bed. Above the discovery place was a balcony, used for the famous balcony scenes of *Romeo and Juliet* (II.2 and III.5), or for the battlements of Richard's castle when he is confronted by Bolingbroke in *Richard II* (III.3). Actors (all parts in the Elizabethan theatre were taken by boys or men) had access to the area beneath the stage; from here, in the 'cellarage', would have come the voice of the ghost of Hamlet's father (*Hamlet*, II.1.150–82).

On these stages there was very little in the way of scenery or props – there was nowhere to store them (there were no wings in this theatre) nor any way to set them up (no tabs across the stage), and, anyway, productions had to be transportable for performance at court or at noble houses. The stage was bare, which is why characters often tell us where they are: there was nothing on the stage to indicate location. It is also why location is so rarely topographical, and much more often symbolic. It suggests a dramatic mood or situation, rather than a place: Lear's barren heath reflects his destitute state, as the storm his emotional turmoil.

None of the plays printed in Shakespeare's lifetime marks act or scene divisions. These have been introduced by later editors, but they should not mislead us into supposing that there was any break in Elizabethan performances such as might happen today while the curtains are closed and the set is changed. The staging of Elizabethan plays was continuous, with the many short 'scenes' of which Shakespeare's plays are often constructed following one after another in quick succession. We have to think of a more fluid, and much faster, production than we are generally used to: in the prologues to *Romeo and Juliet* (line 12) and *Henry VIII* (line 13) Shakespeare speaks of only two hours as the playing time. It is because of this continuous staging and the lack of scenery that characters in Shakespeare's plays often tell the audience what locality the stage represents at different moments. For the same reason, dead bodies had always to be removed by the actors in the course of the play: they cannot get up and walk off.

In 1608 Shakespeare's company, the King's Men, acquired the Blackfriars Theatre, a smaller, rectangular indoor theatre, holding about 700 people, with seats for all the members of the audience, facilities for elaborate stage effects and, because it was enclosed, artificial lighting. It has been suggested that the plays written for this 'private' theatre differed from those written for the Globe, since, as it cost more to go to a private theatre, the audience came from a higher social stratum and demanded the more elaborate and courtly entertainment which Shakespeare's romances provide. However, the King's Men continued to play in the Globe in the summer, using Blackfriars in the winter, and it is not certain that Shakespeare's last plays were written specifically for the Blackfriars Theatre, or first performed there.

READING SHAKESPEARE

Shakespeare's plays were written for this stage, but there is also a sense in which they were written *by* this stage. The material and physical circumstances of their production in such theatres had a profound effect upon the nature of Elizabethan plays. Unless we bear this in mind, we are likely to find them very strange, for we will read with expectations shaped by our own familiarity with modern fiction and modern drama. This is, by and large, realistic; it seeks to persuade us that what we are reading or watching is really happening. This is quite foreign to Shakespeare. If we try to read him like this, we shall find ourselves irritated by the improbabilities of his plot, confused by his chronology, puzzled by locations, frustrated by unanswered questions and dissatisfied by the motivation of the action. The absurd ease with which disguised persons pass through Shakespeare's plays is a case in point: why does no-one recognise people they know so well? There is a great deal of psychological accuracy in Shakespeare's plays, but we are far from any attempt at realism.

The reason is that in Shakespeare's theatre it was impossible to pretend that the audience was not watching a contrived performance. In a modern theatre, the audience is encouraged to forget itself as it becomes absorbed by the action on stage. The worlds of the spectators and of the actors are sharply distinguished by the lighting: in the dark auditorium the audience is passive, silent, anonymous, receptive and attentive; on the lighted stage the actors are active, vocal, demonstrative and dramatic. (The distinction is, of course, still more marked in the cinema.) There is no communication between the two worlds: for the audience to speak would be interruptive; for the actors to address the audience would be to break the illusion of the play. In the Elizabethan theatre, this distinction did not exist, and for two reasons: first, performances took place in the open air and in daylight which illuminated everyone equally; secondly, the spectators were all around the stage (and wealthier spectators actually on it), and were dressed no differently to the actors, who wore contemporary dress. In such a theatre, spectators would be as aware of each other as of the actors; they could not lose their identity in a corporate group, nor could they ever forget that they were spectators at a performance. There was no chance that they could believe 'this is really happening'.

This, then, was communal theatre, not only in the sense that it was going on in the middle of a crowd but in the sense that the crowd joined in. Elizabethan audiences had none of our deference: they did not keep quiet, or arrive on time, or remain for the whole performance. They joined in, interrupted, even getting on the stage. And plays were preceded and followed by jigs and clowning. It was all much more like our experience of a pantomime, and at a pantomime we are fully aware, and are meant to be aware, that we are watching games being played with reality. The conventions of pantomime revel in their own artificiality: the Dame's monstrous false breasts signal that 'she' is a man.

Something very similar is the case with Elizabethan theatre: it utilised its very theatricality. Instead of trying to persuade spectators that they are not in a theatre watching a performance, Elizabethan plays acknowledge the presence of the audience. It is addressed not only by prologues, epilogues and choruses, but in **soliloquies**. There is no realistic reason why characters should suddenly explain themselves to empty rooms, but, of course, it is not an empty room. The actor is surrounded by people. Soliloquies are not addressed to the world of the play: they are for the audience's benefit. And that audience's complicity is assumed: when a character like Prospero declares himself to be invisible, it is accepted that he is. Disguises are taken to be impenetrable, however improbable, and we are to accept impossibly contrived situations, such as barely hidden characters remaining undetected (indeed, on the Elizabethan stage there was nowhere at all they could hide!).

These, then, are plays which are aware of themselves as dramas; in critical terminology, they are **self-reflexive**, commenting upon themselves as dramatic pieces and prompting the audience to think about the theatrical experience. They do this not only through their direct address to the audience but through their fondness for the play-within-a-play (which reminds the audience that the encompassing play is also a play) and their constant use of images from, and allusions to, the theatre. They are fascinated by role playing, by acting, appearance and reality. Things are rarely what they seem, either in comedy (for example, in *A Midsummer Night's Dream*) or tragedy (*Romeo and Juliet*). This offers one way to think about those disguises: they are thematic rather than realistic. Kent's disguise in *Lear* reveals his true, loyal self, while Edmund, who is not disguised, hides his true self. In *As You Like It*, Rosalind is more truly herself disguised as a man than when dressed as a woman.

The effect of all this is to confuse the distinction we would make between 'real life' and 'acting'. The case of Rosalind, for example, raises searching questions about gender roles, about how far it is 'natural' to be womanly or manly: how does the stage, on which a man can play a woman playing a man (and have a man fall in love with him/her!), differ from life, in which we assume the roles we think appropriate to masculine and feminine behaviour? The same is true of political roles: when a Richard II or Lear is so aware of the regal part he is performing, of the trappings and rituals of kingship, their plays raise the uncomfortable possibility that the answer to the question, what consititutes a successful king, is simply: a good actor. Indeed, human life generally is repeatedly rendered through the imagery of the stage, from Macbeth's 'Life's but a walking shadow, a poor player / That struts and frets his hour upon the stage / And then is heard no more …' (V.5.23–5) to Prospero's paralleling of human life to a performance which, like the globe (both world and theatre) will end (IV.I.146–58). When life is a fiction, like this play, or this play is a fiction like life, what is the difference? 'All the world's a stage …' (*As You Like It*, II.7.139).

PART SIX

CRITICAL HISTORY

RECEPTION AND EARLY CRITICAL VIEWS

We know more about the early reception of *The Tempest* than we do about many of Shakespeare's plays. It was first performed on 1 November 1611, in Whitehall in the presence of King James I. We do not have any records of how the play was received but the subject matter was topical (James was interested in colonisation and had sponsored Sir Walter Raleigh's last trip to South America) and it was selected for another courtly performance in 1613 to celebrate the marriage of James I's daughter, Elizabeth, to Prince Frederick of Bohemia. When Shakespeare's works were collected and published in 1623, *The Tempest* appears first, a fact that may suggest its popularity at the time. And it has remained popular ever since, attracting not only audiences but painters too, including Richard Dadd, George Romney and Henry Townsend.

The plot of *The Tempest* may be divorced from real life in that its chief character, Prospero, is a magician who can control the spirits of air, earth, fire and water and who can use spells to put Miranda to sleep, to punish Caliban and to remedy old wrongs. The play presupposes a knowledge of and interest in the supernatural, an interest that was probably more widespread in Shakespeare's day than in our own. It is worth noting, for example, that King James I wrote a treatise on magic in 1603. And yet, in spite of the unreality of the setting and of Prospero's mysterious powers, the play deals with themes like love, sin and repentance, colonial contacts, themes that relate to the world of reality and have as much significance now as they had when Shakespeare wrote.

CRITICAL HISTORY

Shakespeare's plays, like all drama, fell out of favour during the Cromwellian period and there is no record of any production for half a century. In 1667, John Dryden (1631-1700) and William D'Avenant (1606-68) adapted *The Tempest* for a post-Restoration audience. They created a series of new characters so that Caliban and Ariel could have sexual partners; they gave Miranda a sister, Dorinda, and Prospero was given a ward, Hippolito, a young man who had never seen a woman. This version concentrates on the problems and humour associated with sexual jealousy, although it introduces a note of political satire in the quarrels between Stephano and Trinculo.

In the early eighteenth century, *The Tempest* was regarded as a delightful but far-fetched fantasy, although many writers, including Joseph Addison (1672-1719) and Samuel Johnson (1709-84), were impressed by the depiction of Caliban and preferred the original text to the Dryden and D'Avenant version. Towards the second part of this century, critics began to comment on the romance and imaginative extravagance of the play and the poet Samuel Taylor Coleridge (1772-1834) wrote several essays on it, suggesting it was, in a very real sense, a dramatic poem whose themes were too profound to be understood properly from watching a performance.

In the nineteenth century, some performances were romantic and others delighted in the technical advances of the contemporary stage. The Charles Keane production of 1856 is an example of the latter. It made use of '140 operatives' nightly to work the elaborate machinery and create the stage effects favoured by early Victorian theatregoers.

The New Shakespeare Society was founded in 1873 and, under its influence, attempts were made to produce the play as Shakespeare intended. Producers broke away from much of the technical extravaganza and staged *The Tempest* as a realistic drama rather than as a romantic poem. There was, however, a tendency to concentrate on an idealised maturity that stressed the value of wise old age.

Early twentieth-century critics, such as Lytton Strachey, tended to stress a cynical and disillusioned interpretation. They suggested that *The Tempest* failed to satisfy because it was the product of a jaded genius. The second half of this century has seen a re-appraisal of the play. Many productions reveal the power of the language, the subtlety of much of the characterisation, the richness of meaning, and the complexity of the themes.

Throughout the period between Shakespeare's time and ours, however, few critics or audiences have failed to be impressed by the characters of Prospero and Caliban. Prospero may be depicted as a god-like figure, meting out an ill-understood justice, or as a despotic coloniser; Caliban may be seen as an example of the Rousseauesque 'noble savage', or as a representative of a subjugated people, bound in body but free in spirit. Whatever interpretation a producer chooses, the language allows for a degree of latitude. We can pick out certain characteristics but, even when we have listed them exhaustively, we still cannot pigeon-hole them because they are like real people in their ability to surprise us, even when we think we have plumbed their depths.

CONTEMPORARY APPROACHES: DIFFERENT READINGS

The Tempest resembles *The Merchant of Venice* in that modern audiences tend to react differently from Shakespeare's contemporaries to Caliban and Shylock. For us, living after colonisation and the Holocaust and aware of the dangers of prejudice, it is impossible not to sympathise with these characters, although there is evidence that many of Shakespeare's contemporaries would not have shared this sympathy. Perhaps, it is a tribute to Shakespeare's greatness as a dramatist and to his sensitivity as a person, that the plays themselves allow us to empathise with both Caliban and Shylock.

Part seven

Broader perspectives

Further reading

There are many texts on Shakespeare that the interested student might enjoy but the following list will prove helpful.

Texts of *The Tempest*

The text of *The Tempest* that was published in the First **Folio** of 1623 is comparatively free from errors or problem sections and so most modern editions are based on it. This is one play, therefore, where you can choose almost any edition of the text although the Arden, the Cambridge, the Heinemann, the Longman and the Penguin editions are particularly useful. There are also recordings available if you want to hear good readings of the play, together with the use of authentic period music for the songs. Lastly, for those with access to the World Wide Web, you might like to do a search on this play. You will find excellent data on performances and productions by requesting, for example, 'shakespeare+the tempest' and some interesting background information on paintings inspired by *The Tempest* on such a website as:

www.cc.emory.edu/ENGLISH/classes ... speare_Illustrated/Romney.Tempest.html

General

Charles Barber, *The English Language: A Historical Introduction*, Cambridge University Press, 1993

An excellent survey of the history and development of the English language

Michael D. Bristol, *Big-Time Shakespeare*, Routledge, 1997

This book evaluates the dispute concerning Shakespeare's place in the **canon** of English and European literature. Bristol is particularly useful in describing the richness of the original texts as dramatic products of a particular person at a particular time, and yet of showing how they have been interpreted – and sometimes manipulated – by subsequent generations

Winifred Friedman, *Boydell's Shakespeare Gallery*, Garland, 1976

Examines some of the paintings used to represent Shakespeare's plays and characters

Terence Hawkes, *Alternative Shakespeares*: Volumes 1 and 2, Routledge, 1987 and 1997

These books examine received opinions on Shakespeare and show how traditional criticism can be examined best chronologically. Volume 2 has some relevant points to make on Caliban in relation to racism and colonialism

Jonathan Hope, *The Authorship of Shakespeare's Plays: A Sociolinguistic Study*, Cambridge University Press, 1994

Hope provides an up-to-date evaluation of techniques for judging which plays were written by Shakespeare and which might be regarded as works of collaboration

D.G. James, *The Dream of Prospero*, Clarendon Press, 1968

David Lindley, *Court Masques*, Oxford World's Classics Drama Series, 1995

Useful background to the origin and development of the **masque genre**; particularly good on their music

Octave Mannoni, *Prospero and Caliban: The Psychology of Colonisation*, Methuen, 1956

This book is old now but it still provides an excellent discussion of the relationship between Caliban and Prospero and the sociological implications of colonisation

Alden T. Vaughan and Virginia Mason Vaughan, *Shakespeare's Caliban: A Cultural History*, Cambridge University Press, 1991

This is well worth reading for its insights into contemporary attitudes to colonisation and indigenous peoples. The book chronicles the background against which Caliban was created and looks at how subsequent generations have regarded him

Marina Warner, *Indigo or Mapping the Waters*, Vintage, 1993

Marina Warner's feminist novel is, in part, a reworking of *The Tempest*, and attempts to give a voice and a sense of history to those like Sycorax, Ariel and Caliban, who may be said to have been inadequately represented in Shakespeare's play

If you are interested in the texts that may have inspired Shakespeare to write *The Tempest*, you might like to study the following:

Sylvester Jourdain, *Discovery of the Bermudas*, 1610

M. de Montaigne, 'Of the Caniballes', essay published in 1603

William Strachey, *True Reportory of the Wrack*, written in 1610 but published in 1625 in *Purchas His Pilgrimes*, xix, 5–72

CHRONOLOGY

World events	Shakespeare's life	Literature and the arts
1492 Columbus sails to America		
		1513 Niccolò Machiavelli, *The Prince*
1534 Henry VIII breaks with Rome and declares himself head of the Church of England		
1556 Archbishop Cranmer burnt at the stake		
1558 Elizabeth I accedes to throne		
	1564 Born in Stratford-upon-Avon	
		1565-7 Arthur Golding, *Ovid's Metamorphosis* (translated from Latin)
1568 Mary Queen of Scots taken prisoner by Elizabeth I		
1570 Elizabeth I excommunicated by Pope Pius V		
1571 The Battle of Lepanto		
1577 Francis Drake sets out on round the world voyage		
1582 Outbreak of the Plague in London	**1582** Marries Anne Hathaway	
	1583 His daughter, Susanna, is born	
1584 Raleigh's sailors land in Virginia		
	1585 His twins, Hamnet and Judith, born	
1587 Execution of Mary Queen of Scots after implication in plot to murder Elizabeth I		**1587** Christopher Marlowe, *Tamburlaine the Great*
	late 1580s-early 90s Probably writes *Henry VI (Parts I, II, III)* and *Richard III*	
	c1585-92 Moves to London	
1588 The Spanish Armada defeated		
1589 Accession of Henri IV to French throne		
1592 Plague in London closes theatres	**1592** Writes *The Comedy of Errors*	
	1593 Writes *Titus Andronicus, The Taming of the Shrew*	
	1594 onwards Writes exclusively for the Lord Chamberlain's Men; writes *Two Gentlemen of Verona, Love's Labours Lost, Richard II*	
	1595 Writes *Romeo and Juliet, A Midsummer Night's Dream*	
1596 Drake perishes on expedition to West Indies	**1596** Hamnet dies; William granted coat of arms	

World events	Shakespeare's life	Literature and the arts
	1598 Writes *Much Ado About Nothing*	**1598** Christopher Marlowe, *Hero and Leander*
	1599 Buys share in the Globe Theatre; writes *Julius Caesar, As You Like It, Twelfth Night*	
	1600 *The Merchant of Venice* printed	
	1600-1 Writes *Hamlet, The Merry Wives of Windsor*	
	1601 Writes *Troilus and Cressida*	
	1602 Writes *All's Well That Ends Well*	
1603 Death of Queen Elizabeth I	**1603** onwards His company enjoys patronage of James I as The King's Men	**1603** Michel Eyquem de Montaigne, *Of Cannibals,* translated by John Florio
	1604 *Othello* performed; writes *Measure for Measure*	
1605 Discovery of Guy Fawkes's plot to blow up the Houses of Parliament	**1605** First version of *King Lear*	**1605** Cervantes, *Don Quijote de la Mancha*
	1606 Writes *Macbeth*	
	1606-7 Probably writes *Antony and Cleopatra*	
	1607 Writes *Coriolanus, Timon of Athens*	
	1608 Writes *Pericles*; The King's Men acquire Blackfriars Theatre for winter performances	
1609 Galileo constructs first astronomical telescope	**1609** Becomes part-owner of the new Blackfriars Theatre	
1610 Henri IV of France assassinated; William Harvey discovers circulation of blood; Galileo observes Saturn for the first time		**1610** Pamphlet published entitled *A Discovery of the Bermudas, other wise called the Ile of Divels*
	1611 *Cymbeline, The Winter's Tale* and *The Tempest* performed	
1612 Last burning of heretics in England		
	1613 The Globe Theatre burns down	
	1616 Dies	
1618 Raleigh executed for treason; Thirty Years War begins in England		
		1622 Birth of French dramatist Molière

LITERARY TERMS

Most of the unusual terms used in this book have been explained in context but the following brief glossary may be helpful:

action in drama, action is often subdivided into: external action, referring to the physical events that occur; internal action, referring to the characters' thoughts and feelings; and stage action, referring to events that actually occur on the stage

acts major divisions of a play. In Greek drama, the major divisions were signalled by the participation of the chorus. Many Latin plays, including those of Seneca, were divided into five acts. Shakespeare followed this tradition

allegory the use of people, objects and events in such a way that more than one level of meaning is conveyed. Sometimes, allegories are used to convey a moral or a series of moral lessons

alliteration the repetition of initial consonant sounds in stressed syllables for emphasis or decorative effect, for example, 'You **n**ymphs, called **N**aiads' (IV.1.128)

anachronism assignment of an attitude, event, person or thing to a place or time when such an attitude, event, person or thing did not exist

aphorism a brief, almost proverbial statement of a piece of wisdom. Gonzalo uses aphorisms almost as much as Polonius does in *Hamlet*

apron stage a stage that projects into the auditorium and cannot easily be framed by curtains

assonance the repetition of the same vowel sound. Assonance is less easy to detect in *The Tempest* than alliteration because the pronunciation of vowels has changed considerably over the last 400 years. We can find an example of it in 'five' and lies': 'Full fathom five thy father lies' (I.2.400)

Bible the 'Bible' is usually considered to be composed of the 39 books of the Old Testament and the Gospels, Epistles, Acts of the Apostles and Revelations of the New Testament

blank verse unrhymed verse. When the lines contain ten syllables with stresses on the second, fourth, sixth, eighth and tenth syllables, they are called 'iambic pentameters':

x / x / x / x / x / (x = unstressed, / = stressed)
So have we all, of joy; for our escape
x / x/ x / x / x /
Is much beyond our loss. Our hint of woe (II.1.2–3)

canon see **critic**

catharsis the Aristotelian concept that tragedy can purge the emotions of members of the audience by evoking feelings of pity for the fate suffered by the protagonists and fear that similar fates might befall them

climax the turning point in the action of a drama

critic a person who passes judgement on the value of a piece of literature. Critics often establish a canon, that is, a set of literary works regarded as the best of their kind in the language

deconstruction an attempt to reveal the partially hidden meanings in a text, especially those that illuminate aspects of its relationship with its social and political context

dénouement the final unravelling of the plot

dramatic irony when the words or actions in a play have a significance more apparent to the audience than to the character

epilogue a concluding statement

figure of speech the non-literal use of language. The most frequently used figures of speech are metaphor (e.g. the sun smiled) and simile (e.g. a face like the sun)

folio a printer's sheet of paper folded so as to make four pages. Shakespeare's First Folio was printed in 1623, seven years after his death

genre literature is often divided into different categories according to form or purpose. The three main categories or 'genres' are drama, poetry and the novel

imagery the use of figurative language for imaginative and emotional reasons

madrigal a short lyric usually dealing with pastoral life or romanticised love. It varies in length between six and thirteen lines and usually has a maximum of three rhymes:

> Where the bee sucks, there suck I.
> In a cowslip's bell I lie (V.1.88ff)

masque Parades involving people wearing masks were relatively common in medieval times. This tradition was developed in the Elizabethan and Jacobean period (c. 1580–1640) and turned into elaborate spectacles called 'masques', a variant spelling of 'masks'. Courtly masques were especially popular towards the end of Elizabeth's reign and during the reign of James I (1603–25). These entertainments made use of elaborate costumes and scenery and frequently involved professional musicians and dancers. The singers and dancers often wore expensive masks

metaphor a comparison where the similarity is assumed, as in I.2.318 when Prospero refers to Caliban as 'thou tortoise' rather than saying 'you are as slow as a tortoise'

metre regulated rhythm

mime a play in which the performers use actions and gestures, rather than words, to convey their meaning

morality plays poetic drama that developed in the Middle Ages. Often abstractions such as 'peace' and 'shame' were personified. These are sometimes distinguished from 'miracle plays', which centred on the legends surrounding saints, and 'mystery plays', which were based on biblical stories

motif a recurring theme. The struggle between brothers may be regarded as a motif in *The Tempest*

nemesis divine punishment for evil deeds

pastoral literature involving a romantic view of rustic life

pentameter a line of verse containing five stressed syllables

plot a series of inter-related incidents used as the framework for a play or a piece of fiction

point of view the outlook of the writer, narrator or character

pun play on words that have several meanings (e.g. 'will') or that sound similar (e.g. 'grace' and 'grease')

quarto a book made up of sheets that have been folded twice so as to produce eight pages on four sheets

rhetoric the rules that underpin the creation of clear, polished and attractive structures

self-reflexive plays that comment on themselves as dramatic pieces

subplot a subordinate story. The actions of Trinculo and Stephano constitute a subplot

symbol an item or activity that has relevance on both the literal and metaphorical levels. A storm can be both literal and representative of human passions

tragicomedy a plot that has the elements of a tragedy but which has a happy ending

unities principles of dramatic development involving action, time and place

AUTHOR OF THIS NOTE

Loreto Todd is Reader in International English at the University of Leeds and Director of the Programme of World English Research. Professor Todd has lectured in many parts of the world and written numerous books, including *The Language of Irish Literature*, *Modern Englishes*, *Words Apart*, *A Dictionary of English Usage* and *Variety in Contemporary English*. She has been Chief Examiner of A-level English and is currently editing a series on *World English*.